A QUIET CORNER IN A LIBRARY

A QUIET CORNER
IN A LIBRARY

By

WILLIAM HENRY HUDSON

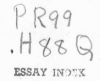
Essay Index Reprint Series

BOOKS FOR LIBRARIES PRESS

FREEPORT, NEW YORK

First published 1915
Reprinted 1968

LIBRARY OF CONGRESS CATALOG CARD NUMBER:

68-16940

PRINTED IN THE UNITED STATES OF AMERICA

PREFACE

THE following papers may best be described perhaps as by-products of the writer's more serious work in literature. They grew naturally out of studies upon which for a good many years past I have been engaged with other ends in view, but they represent the mood of relaxation rather than that of strenuous effort. While I should be sorry to think that they are superficial in the ordinary sense of the word, I would nevertheless ask the reader to remember that they are not offered as exhaustive essays on the subjects with which they deal. The title chosen for the volume at the suggestion of a friend will I hope be understood to indicate something of its general tone and character.

It is perhaps worth while to mention that no portion of the book has hitherto appeared in print. Of the contents individually little needs to be said. The essay on Tom Hood is the expansion of a lecture originally prepared a good many years ago for audiences in California. The remaining papers, which, as will be seen, have many points of connection, are concerned with certain aspects of eighteenth-century literature in which I have long been specially interested. That on Lillo merely touches the fringe of a subject which I am treating at length and in all its bearings, literary and social, in a volume on *George Lillo and the Middle Class Drama of the Eighteenth Century*, now nearing completion.

If I shall have succeeded in transmitting to the reader

PREFACE

of these pages something of the pleasure which I myself experienced in collecting materials for them during
many hours of leisurely wandering in the highways and
byways of literature, I shall be well satisfied.

WILLIAM HENRY HUDSON

London, January, 1915

CONTENTS

ix

PROEM

Old Dick on his favorite cushion
Purrs lazily at the fire;
Jack on his chair is dreaming, I know,
Of his tramp through the rain and the mire;

And from the room adjoining,
Where SHE sits and charms the keys,
Come strains of one of Schumann's
Most magical melodies.

The night has fallen early,
With a welter of wind and rain;
'T is a dismal scene that meets my gaze
Through the blurred window-pane.

So I draw the curtains quickly,
And shut it away from sight,
And turn to my little book-lined world
Of love, and warmth, and light.

O world of pure enchantment,
Where pleasure never palls!
O friends of many times and tongues
Who watch me from the walls!

Your spell is strong upon me! —
Across the driving rain
There are voices calling — calling —
But to-night they call in vain.

Here is my quiet corner,
And my book that waits thereby: —
Now, pray, in the whole of London Town,
Who more happy than I?

A QUIET CORNER IN A LIBRARY

TOM HOOD: "THE MAN, THE WIT, AND THE POET"

I

IT is with an odd feeling of disenchantment, dashed often, I think, with a certain sense of the pathos of things, that from time to time we turn back to the books which were our chosen companions in years gone by. In an idle hour, more by accident, probably, than design, we take from the shelf some volume once deeply cherished for its wit or wisdom, its poetry or romance. How willingly, then, would we renew the old charm! How strangely, how irrevocably, that old charm seems to have fled! We remember with the vividness of yesterday the feelings of rapt admiration and intense sympathy with which we were wont to linger spellbound over those once magic pages. How they glowed and sparkled in those other days! How they clutched us by the very heartstrings! How eloquent they were — how tender -- how beautiful!

1

There is no fascination in the literature we afterwards come to love quite equal to the fascination of those enchanters of our youth. And behold! "whither is fled the visionary gleam? Where is it now, the glory and the dream?" The life has evaporated, the spell has been broken! The chances are that the poetry seems tumid to us; the romance tawdry; the moralizing trite; the humor flat and futile. We shake our wiser heads sadly; and, not without a sigh, we lay the book aside. *Requiescat in pace* — for it is part and parcel of our own dead selves. Let us deal with it gently, as we should deal with the memory of a schoolboy friend into whose willing ear we once poured our heart's secrets, and whom we pass in the street with a formal handshake or half a dozen commonplace words of recognition.

The history of our taste in fiction, for example, will generally exhibit some extraordinary mutations. It is quite true, as the sage Benedick tells us, that "a man loves the meat in his youth that he cannot endure in his age." I recall my own experience. There was the typical case of *Ivanhoe*. Some years ago, while writing a book on Scott, I went through the *Waverley Novels* afresh in the chronological order of their production; and this is how I had to report concerning that

2

prime favorite of my boyhood: "*Ivanhoe* was the first that left with me a distinct feeling of disappointment. I remembered it as rapid, passionate, full of breathless incident and enthralling interest; I found it a superb piece of stucco-work, melodramatic and wholly unreal." Somewhat later, when I began to be interested in philosophical speculations, and Scott failed me a little, I recollect that I was held spellbound by *Ernest Maltravers*, *Alice*, and *Zanoni*. I know perfectly well (I have not looked into them since) that to-day I should regard these books as superficial, pretentious, and overwrought. In my quite early manhood (if I dare to confess it) I derived immense entertainment from the *grisettes* and little *bourgeoisie* of poor old Paul de Kock. I tried one of his novels the other day; it resembled nothing so much as an effervescing drink from which all the fizz had gone. And as for Charles Lever, over whose pages (though I admit that this was in my very callow days) I used to laugh immoderately; well, I recently made an heroic attempt to read through *Charles O'Malley*, in a brand-new edition which I bought expressly for the purpose; and I stuck ignominiously before I was halfway through.

But one grows garrulous when one begins

to talk about oneself, and these reminiscences into which I have wandered are no further to the point. Let me come at once to the matter by which such generalities were in the first instance suggested.

II

The other day I chanced to turn over, for the first time in I will not say how many years, the pages of one of Tom Hood's *Comic Annuals*. It were impertinent for me now to speak of the delicate personal associations which cluster about this book—of the melancholy trains of thought which were started by the grotesque pictures, and the whims and oddities of the letter-press. But perhaps because these certain connections put me, as it were, at a wrong point of view, but also, I am sure, because of a profound change of taste, I read with little amusement, and was even glad to put the volume again in its place on the shelf. A certain faint odor, as of something faded, seemed to exhale from its pages. *Tempora mutantur, nos et mutamur in illis!* Did I once — I could not help asking myself — think that these pages contained the very quintessence of wit—the finest flavor of jesting? On the whole—I was fain to confess it— notwithstanding their frequent flashes and

4

coruscations, they now struck me as labored, heavy, mechanical.

Yet in such a case as this we must be on our guard lest revulsion of feeling should carry us too far. Because in later life the operatic mediævalism of *Ivanhoe* is realized in all its unsoundness; because the atrabilious eruptions of *Lara* and *The Corsair* are no longer accepted as giving the profoundest reading of life in the most brilliant poetry the world has ever seen; because the perfervid rhapsodies of *Queen Mab* seem windy and meretricious, we do not therefore pass a hasty and sweeping judgment upon Scott, and Byron, and Shelley, or dream of challenging their title to the high place assigned to them in English letters. And if any one takes the trouble to examine the entire work of Tom Hood, he will soon discover that it is not on the strength of his *Comic Annuals* that he is held in kindly remembrance by all lovers of good literature. Had he left these alone behind him, he himself would have passed away with the temporary fashions to which he catered. But as a matter of fact, though they still, I suppose, bulk large in popular estimation of him, such things are really clogs upon his fame. We know that they belong not to literature, but to journalism; that they were actually mere potboilers, produced year by year, in days of pain and sorrow and struggle, for the immediate and urgent purpose of keeping house and home together. If we must dismiss them as unworthy of any serious attention, let us do so, then, as gently as possible, and say no more than we need about it.

But meanwhile there are other parts of Hood's work which we cannot and must not allow to pass into oblivion with them. There is one searching question which we may fairly put in regard to any writer, be he small or great — a question upon the answer to which must ultimately depend the view that we take of him as a real personality, a permanent living figure in literary history. Whatever his work, his vital power, his temporary success or failure, did he or did he not do something which other men have not done at all, or not done nearly as well? Press that question well home, abide by the answer as a test, and you will find that there are plenty of writers who made a brilliant showing in the eyes of their contemporaries, who even contrive to fill considerable space in the chronicles, if only as certain people of importance in their own day, who none the less might drop out of memory without leaving much of a gap by their disappearance. And there are others.

6

on the contrary, who, superficially regarded, may seem of far slighter stature, whose loss would none the less be a very real loss, because it would leave us the poorer by something which no one else has given us—something altogether personal with them. To this latter class Tom Hood belongs. Judge him otherwise how we may, we must all of us recognize that, when the perishable parts of his over-voluminous production are brushed aside, there remain certain things which stand by themselves—things of a kind that only Tom Hood has written—that only Tom Hood could write.

III

Before we turn to these things, however, let us briefly run over the story of Hood's career of ill-health, struggle, and strenuous activity. If it be indeed a general fact (as we are continually told) that the lives of men of letters make the saddest of all biographies, the life of Hood was certainly not one of the happy exceptions which may be taken to prove the rule. Yet we read its melancholy record with profound satisfaction; it brings us in touch with an essentially noble and lovable man, and, no matter what the external conditions, it is always a pleasure and an inspiration to come into contact with such an one.

7

Like his friend Charles Lamb, whom in so many ways he resembled, Hood met trouble, anxiety, and suffering with a cheerful courage which puts to shame the heroic posturings and grandiloquence of many who have made capital out of affliction, and posed before the world as great souls tried by the fiery ordeals of the gods. What a completely satisfactory contrast he provides, for example, with his brilliant contemporary, that flabby moralist of transcendent genius, who made up by torrents of eloquent preaching for weaknesses of practice which rendered his career a spectacle alike for sorrow and for contempt! Always kindly, thoughtful, sympathetic, buoyant in stormiest waters, with a ready jest even in dire emergencies, and a steady hold upon the fundamentals of a simple faith, Hood stands before us as a man whom we may indeed pity from the bottom of our hearts, but for whom, after all, our feelings are less of commiseration than of warm admiration and high personal regard.

He was born on May 23, 1799, and first saw the light—or, as he suggests, possibly the fog—of day in the city of London; being thus able to exult in the fact that, as a genuine Cockney, he could rank himself with Milton, Gray, Defoe, Pope, Byron, Lamb, Keats, and many another town-born author whose fame has "triumphed over the Bills of Mortality." He was one of six children, three of whom—and the fact is ominous — early succumbed to pulmonary trouble inherited from the mother's side. His father, a Scotsman by birth, was at the time of Tom's appearance on this planet a partner in the firm of Vernon, Hood, and Sharp, publishers in the Poultry. He was also himself — as many publishers are not — of a literary turn of mind, and actually perpetrated a couple of novels, long since forgotten even by name. In this way Hood accounts for the "dash of ink" that was undoubtedly in his blood, and for the facility with which, like a latter-day Faustus, he presently sold his soul to "that minor Mephistopheles, the Printer's Devil."

In his rambling *Reminiscences,* written toward the close of his life, he deals at considerable length with the events and surroundings of childhood; but delightful as his recollections are, we must not here attempt to follow them in detail. It will suffice to say that, having acquired the rudiments of learning under the care of a couple of maiden ladies rejoicing (if they did rejoice, which seems unlikely) in the astonishing name of Hogs-flesh, and having to that extent become, at the very outset of his career, a good Baconian, he was presently sent, first to a suburban boarding school (the "Clapham Academy" of his inimitable ode), and then for a short time to a day school in Clerkenwell. Here his education—such as it was—closed prematurely, it would appear, with the closing of the school, or perhaps more correctly, with its rather sudden transformation from a boys' school into a Ladies' Academy.

He had thus far contrived to pick up as much as a quick boy of his age—he was about fourteen—would be likely to appropriate for himself from such instruction—a little Latin, a fair knowledge of English grammar, French enough to enable him by and by to earn his first literary fee by revising a translation of *Paul et Virginie* for the press, and a good practical grasp of figures. It scarcely needs to be added, however, that Hood's gains at school represented only a very small fragment of his real education. His own wit, alertness, and early developed love of books provided the rest. Even the lightest of his writings will be found to testify to a wonderfully wide and accurate knowledge of English literature. This he must have obtained for himself by his voracious reading during many happy hours, then and in after years.

At this point, a family friend undertook to

do Mrs. Hood, already a widow, a good turn,
by introducing her only surviving son to the
mysteries of commerce. The boy, therefore,
took his place on a counting house stool,
which "served occasionally for a Pegasus on
three legs, every foot of course being a dactyl
or a spondee." This simply means that, like
the rest of his kind, he often amused himself
by penning stanzas when he should have been,
if not engrossing, at least engrossed in something else. Or, as he himself puts it, his quill
would now and then "turn vagrant," and
refresh itself, after the severe toils of daybook
or ledger, by "stray dips into the Castalian
pool." The result was the most appalling
confusion:

"Now double entry — now a flowery trope —
  Mingling poetic honey with trade wax —
Blugg Brothers — Milton — Grote and Prescott — Pope
Bristles — and Hogg — Glyn, Mills, and Halifax —
Rogers — and Towgood — Hemp — the Bard of Hope —
Barilla — Byron — Tallow — Burns — and Flax!"

It will be anticipated that, under these circumstances, his devotion to the ledger should
prove of brief duration; there was, in Slender's
immortal phrase, no great love between them
at the beginning, and it pleased Heaven to
decrease it on further acquaintance.

But the true cause of his retirement from

commercial affairs was not the superior attraction of poetry, but something far more prosaic. His health gave out; his constitution proved unequal to the strain of office confinement; his appetite failed; and in the general bankruptcy which followed, his principal creditor, the stomach, received only an ounce in the pound. By so much sitting, the doctors told him—at least, this is Hood's way of paraphrasing their warning—he was hatching a whole brood of complaints. Change of air was recommended; and he was, therefore, shipped off, as per advice, in a Scotch smack, to his father's relatives in Dundee.

Here he remained, it would seem, about three years, returning to London in 1818, apparently fully set up in health by the rugged outdoor life he had been leading. In the light of after events, however, we can see clearly enough that this threatened illness, barely warded off, was the first manifestation of constitutional weaknesses which were presently to cause so much of the tragedy of his life. He did not now go back to business, but determined to put to account his remarkable deftness with the pencil by making art his profession. He therefore entered the studio of a maternal uncle, Robert Sands, the engraver, and, after an apprenticeship of a couple of

years, began work for himself. The time and
energy devoted to this pursuit were by no
means wasted, for his pictorial skill was afterwards made profitable in the always amusing,
and often exceedingly clever, illustrations
which did so much for the popularity of his
Whims and Oddities and *Comic Annuals*.
There is thus more of epigram than of sober
truth in his own remark that, like Pope's
"tape-tied curtains," he was never meant to
draw; for draw he did, and so successfully,
that he drew not only pictures but public
attention.

None the less, it was not in art that he was
to find his real career. While he was working
with the engraver's style, the pen continued
to exercise its wonted fascination, and verse-
spinning was carried on with ever increasing
delight. At length, by what looks like the
happiest of accidents, he was induced to abandon design, and to make the Muse, with whom
hitherto he had merely flirted, his companion
for life. Changes in the management of the
London Magazine caused that then well known
periodical to pass into the hands of some friends
of his own. They offered him a place on the
staff; with the result that, at two-and-twenty,
Hood found himself installed as sub-editor
of a thriving journal and, in virtue of that office,

a figure of some distinction in the metropolitan literary world of the time.

Hood carried into his new work a zeal which showed that the bowl had at last found its natural bias; he took articles, he says, like a candidate for Holy Orders, and accepted every printer's proof as if it had been a proof of personal regard. Of his relations with the magazine's prominent contributors — with Cary, Proctor, Cunningham, many-tongued Bowring, Hazlitt, Talfourd, Horace Smith, and many another, and above all with dear Charles Lamb — we get interesting glimpses in the literary annals of the period. But what concerns us mainly now is the development of his own genius under the favoring influences of his changed environment. Of course, the larger part of his energy was absorbed by the taxing routine labors of his position; but meanwhile, the rapid ripening of his imaginative powers was unmistakably proved by the poems which from time to time he now published in the *London's* pages.

He had, among other friendships, formed a close intimacy with a young man whose sister he afterwards married — John Hamilton Reynolds, well known to every reader as the special confidant and adviser of Keats. It was through Reynolds that Hood came under

the spell of the genius of that brilliant and ill-
starred youth who about that time had died
in Rome, leaving who shall venture to say
what magnificent promises unfulfilled. As
the loving disciple of Keats, though not by
any means as a servile imitator—for his own
temper and manner were too original for that—
Hood produced his *Lycus the Centaur*, the
Ode to Autumn, and other poems, all marked
by a richness of fancy and a sensuous beauty
of language which frequently remind us of
the young master himself. Presently repub-
lished, with other verse of the same order,
but with a fuller and more certain quality of
art, these poems fell from the press almost
unnoticed and, even when noticed at all,
hardly anywhere rated at their real worth.
We wonder, looking back, at their failure, because it is in virtue of just these productions
that the historian of literature now speaks
of Hood as, in all essentials, the truest of
English poets in the years immediately preceding the rise of Tennyson. It may indeed
be urged that though to-day we fully recognize
the shortsightedness of Hood's contemporaries, these poems are even now as little read
as when they were first issued. But the reason
for this further neglect is not to be found in
any doubt concerning their merits, but rather

in the immense popularity of Hood's later productions — a popularity long disastrous to his poetic fame. He was soon to become generally known as a fun-maker of unrivaled powers and seemingly ulnimited resources — as a fellow of infinite jest and most excellent fancy. And when once a man gets publicly accepted as a wit, he is lucky indeed if, out of the hundreds of folk whose laughter he has stirred, there are ten who will ever show themselves willing to treat him seriously again.

As early as 1825 he opened the vein which, for good or evil, in season and out of season, he was henceforth to work with extraordinary industry and success, when in collaboration with Reynolds, now his brother-in-law, he put forth a little volume of *Odes and Addresses to Great People*. The quality of this collection is perhaps best indicated by the fact that Coleridge, finding no author's name on the title page, wrote directly to Charles Lamb, insisting that it must be his, Lamb's, work, because, first, of the excellence of the puns, and secondly, because of the absence of anything harsh or unkind in the personalities of which the book was made up. Three editions quickly sold out, and Hood awoke to realize that if literature were to be made to pay, it must be literature of the kind in which he had suddenly discovered his unique power. Henceforward he must be mainly the comic man— and the comic man he continued for the most part to be to the very end of his life.

And, indeed, what could he now do, save accept as graciously as possible what seemed like a ruling of fate? He was already a married man; he had given, as Bacon has it, hostages to fortune; and the risks that commonly attend matrimony were in his case multiplied by fragile health, and lack of any income beyond what he could earn by his pen. It is well enough for the critic, viewing the matter in the abstract, to set up high standards of art, and to condemn poor Hood for the prostitution of his powers; but *his* problem was not an abstract, but a grimly concrete, one; and can we venture to blame him if, in the circumstances, he turned aside from serious poetry as a luxury of production in which he could no longer afford to indulge, to another sort of enterprise which at least promised something like a substantial return?

And let us at this point pause long enough to make sure of the true bearings of any adverse judgment we may feel obliged to pass upon much of the hack work which Hood now set himself to do. It is hard, after all, to deal harshly with a man who devoted himself to the task of making us laugh; who, as a fact, does often make us laugh, and whose merriment is nearly always clean, wholesome, and kindly. Our modern world is earnest and strenuous and somber enough in all conscience, and I for one am always ready to welcome a little honest fooling as a very delectable relief.

Our regret in Hood's case, then, is, first, that his everlasting comic journalism so exhausted his energies that the poet in him was practically — though happily not altogether — killed by the funny man; and secondly, that (as with every professional jester, whose humor has to be manufactured to order, even at the least opportune times) much of his output was necessarily labored, mechanical, ineffective. No one — least of all a man of Hood's melancholy temperament, harassed by physical weakness and tormented by financial anxieties — can always command a smile; alas for those who, when the smile does not come of itself, are compelled to force the best imitation of it, for the result of their contortions is often nothing but a grin! That there is overmuch of the grin in Hood's humorous writings it would be idle to deny. We feel the deliberation, the set purpose, with which he must have gone to work to fabricate many of his sketches and poems. Go to!—we can hear him say—our minor Mephistopheles is at one door, and the butcher and baker are at the other; it behooves me to be funny. And he is accordingly funny through the required number of pages—yes, even though his heart is wrung with anxiety and his body racked with pain. If, then, we may sometimes find the fooling impotent, the pathos of the fooling is never so. It is, moreover, only fair to add that, given the conditions of its production, the marvel is that Hood's humorous journalism, year in, year out, should have been as light and fresh and varied as was actually the case; and that, taking one crop of wit with another, he should so often have contrived to be, in his own phrase, merry and wise instead of merry and otherwise. One other point must not be lost sight of. "We have laughed often at folly and sometimes at wisdom," says Lucan to Rabelais, in Lord Lyttleton's brilliant dialogue. It is to Hood's credit that he kept his laughter for folly. Like Artemus Ward, too, he scorned to secure a cheap effect by descents into indecency and profanity. He recognized always—what some of our latter-day would-be wits might do well to remember—that a joke which depends on indecency or profanity had better not be made at all.

Here, at any rate, we have Hood fully committed to a way in literature which was now to be considered, by the larger reading public, as peculiarly his own. A couple of series of *Whims and Oddities*, containing some of his most characteristic things in their particular kind, appeared in 1826 and 1827; and then, amid a good deal of other work which does not now call for even passing notice, he produced, in 1829, the first of those *Comic Annuals* which — a gigantic feat, when one comes to think of it — he kept up single-handed, illustrations as well as letter-press, for nine successive years. Meanwhile the other side of his genius found from time to time memorable, if all too infrequent, expression. Such poems as *Eugene Aram*, the *Plea of the Midsummer Fairies*, and later — for we may anticipate a little — the *Haunted House* and the *Bridge of Sighs*, bore ample testimony to the fact that the irrepressible punster was still a master of delicate fancy and tragic passion.

But in the years during which the *Comic Annuals* regularly ministered to the Christmas amusement of an ever-widening public, the clouds were gathering thicker and darker about Hood's own life. In 1834 the failure of a publishing house plunged him into difficulties from which, to the very end, he never

completely extricated himself. Refusing, like
Scott, to shield himself behind the Bankruptcy
Act, he made over to his creditors what little
property he had, and, in the hope of presently
righting himself, took the desperate course
of mortgaging his brain to his publishers. A
year later, Mrs. Hood fell seriously ill. By
this time, too, Hood himself, like his family
and friends, realized that he was under the
doom of a disease, the progress of which might
indeed be arrested temporarily by care and
(if that were possible) release from worry, but
whose fatal issue was a question only of a
little shorter or a little longer delay.

Strange circumstances, these, in which to
find the great maker of laughter, the punctual
producer of quip and pun and whimsical
fancy for a public whose appetite for such
things had grown by what it fed on! Mainly
in the hope of economizing his slender resources,
Hood now took his family to the Continent,
where they lived for five years. If any hope
had been entertained that change of air and
scene might prove beneficial to Hood himself,
it had soon to be abandoned. Unceasing
toil as a mere bookseller's galley slave, and
constant anxiety about his wife's condition
combined to render his courageous fight for
life a struggle against overwhelming odds.

And still the *Comic Annuals* made their punctual appearance; and still the world laughed. Alas, poor Yorick!

When by and by Hood returned to England, it was with health completely and hopelessly shattered. Yet with all his old steady pluck and cheerfulness, he took up the burden of life anew, rejoicing in a slight gleam of sunshine through the breaking clouds. For two years he was in receipt of a regular, if not very princely, salary as editor of Colburn's *New Monthly Magazine,* having succeeded in that capacity another wit of fine powers but strikingly different character—poor Theodore Hook, then recently dead.

In January, 1844, he started a periodical of his own, only to discover within a few months that his constitution could not possibly stand the tremendous double strain of editorial responsibility and productive effort. In June of that year the readers of the magazine were informed in a few paragraphs of unmistakable import, of the precarious condition of its leader and chief support. "It is with feelings of the deepest concern," ran part of the notice, "that we acquaint our subscribers and the public with the circumstances that have, during the past month, deprived the magazine of the invaluable services of its editor. A

22

severe attack of the disorder to which he has long been subject . . . has in the course of a few weeks reduced Mr. Hood to a state of such extreme debility and exhaustion that during several days fears were entertained for his life. Nevertheless, up to Thursday, the 23d, he did not relinquish the hope that he should have strength to continue in the present number the novel which he began in the last. On the same evening, sitting up in bed, he tried to invent and sketch a few comic designs, but even this effort exceeded his strength, and was followed by the wandering delirium of utter nervous exhaustion. Next morning, his medical advisers declared that the repetition of any such attempt, at that critical period of his illness, might cost him his life."

He rallied, but the attack was really the beginning of the end. At the same time, his poetic genius, instead of sinking beneath the burden of bodily infirmity, burst out suddenly with fresh and wonderful power. In the Christmas number of *Punch*, 1843, appeared the famous *Song of the Shirt*; and this was followed, at brief intervals, by the equally famous *Bridge of Sighs*, the *Haunted House*, and the *Lay of the Laborer*. What is remarkable about these productions—apart from their imaginative vigor and their technical

3   23

perfection—is the nobly human spirit by which they are pervaded. Referring to the cardiac hypertrophy which was one of his serious symptoms, Hood himself said that though an enlarged heart was certainly inconvenient, it was better to have an enlarged heart than a contracted one. It was indeed the man's large heart — his broad and deep sympathies — which inspired these last of his poems. It would seem that, as the darkness of the night wherein no one can work closed rapidly about him, his realization of the toils and sufferings of others grew more and more intense. The hand of death was upon him, but he thought less of himself than of those outcasts of civilization to a sense of whose tragedy he sought to stir the world's sluggish conscience — the half-starved seamstress in her garret, the despairing girl seeking a suicide's escape from misery in the black flowing stream.

In the issue of his magazine for February, 1845, appeared a couple of simple, but in their very simplicity wonderfully pathetic, stanzas in which the poet spoke of his approaching death:

"Farewell, Life, my senses swim,
All the world is growing dim,
Thronging shadows cloud the light
Like the advent of the night.

Colder, colder, colder still
Upward steals a vapor chill.
Strong the earthy odor grows—
I smell the mold above the rose.

"Welcome, Life! the spirit strives!
Strength returns and hope revives!
Cloudy fears and shapes forlorn
Fly like shadows at the morn.
O'er the earth there comes a bloom,
Sunny light for sullen gloom,
Warm perfume for vapor cold—
I smell the rose above the mold!"

Three months later—on May 3, 1845—
Hood died. It is said that almost at the last
he remarked to a friend—the ruling passion
strong in death—that he was really dying to
please the undertaker, who wished to urn
(earn) a lively Hood (livelihood). He was
buried in Kensal Green Cemetery, and beneath
the bust which forms part of the memorial
afterwards erected by public subscription, is
inscribed, according to his own express wish,
the brief but sufficient epitaph: "He sang the
Song of the Shirt." Was he not right in
believing that the memory of that song would
be cherished in every warm heart so long as
love and sympathy endure? "Ah," said
Dickens to his friend Forster after visiting
Venice, "when I saw those palaces, how I
thought that to leave one's hand upon the

time—lastingly upon the time—with one tender touch for the mass of toiling people that nothing could obliterate, would be to lift oneself above the dust of all the doges in their graves, and stand upon a giant's staircase that Samson could not overthrow!"

We are justified in classing Hood among those who are secure of this kind of immortality.

IV

Without such an insight into Hood's life and character as in the foregoing sketch I have tried to give, it would be impossible to deal fairly with his work. The abstract principle that the artist is simply what he does — that all we are finally concerned with is his actual achievement, taken just as it stands — may for the present safely be left to those who care for literature only on the æsthetic side. Those of us who love it as an expression of the human spirit, its experiences and adventures, its successes and its failures, will always think instinctively of the man behind the book. Hood's, at least, is surely one of those cases in which a writer's production gains vastly in interest and significance by being connected directly with his personality and career. By so regarding it, we are at once able, first, to

26

understand why so much of his writing falls sadly short of the best that was in him, and then (dismissing this merely mortal part of his output) to apprehend the real power and meaning of the still considerable portion which remains.

For present purposes we may deal with Hood's work as it naturally divides itself under the three general heads of comic, serious, and serio-comic. This is only a rough classification, it is true, but it will serve. First, then, let us turn to the poems in which we hear the tinkle of the bells on the jester's cap.

As a humorist pure and simple, Hood, though he showed great versatility, was undoubtedly, like many humorists of his generation, most at home in the domain of broad farce. His most original achievements, however, depend for their success upon the amazing fertility of his verbal wit. As a punster and master of equivoque, he is still without a serious rival; when the quantity and general quality of his work in this direction are taken into account, he stands out among his competitors like Triton among the minnows. Of course, we may make what charges we like against the pun: we may call it the cheapest form of joking, protest that it is possible only through a poverty of language of which nothing but perverse ingenuity would seek to take advantage; and even denounce it, with the Great Cham himself, as an outward and visible sign of inward and moral degradation. Or if we do not go quite so far as this, we may still urge that the pun is at best a luxury, to be used sparingly, and never abused. It has often been pointed out that the essence of any kind of true joke is its unexpectedness (which, by the way, is the reason, according to Mr. Zangwill, why we are so delighted when we find ourselves laughing over anything in *Punch*). Unexpectedness is certainly, as Edgar Allan Poe remarked, the essence of the pun as a form of jesting. It should come suddenly, and with a shock of surprise to us; to force it into habitual and regular service is to destroy its effectiveness.

Yet when punning is the thing which it became in Hood's hands, I am afraid the criticism is to some extent disarmed. If the charm of suddenness and unexpectedness is gone, we marvel the more at the punctuality of the stroke; and this punctuality yields us, in occasional moods at any rate, something of the satisfaction which the exhibition of complete dexterity in any field seldom fails to afford. Analyzed carefully, we may insist, the whole affair looks unpleasantly like a trick. But, then, what a trick it is! Beyond this, we must note the extraordinary perfection of the results. The best of Hood's puns — they may be reckoned by hundreds — may be regarded as absolute models in their kind. Illustrations come without number and without seeking. We remember the unfortunate soldier on the battlefield speaking of his fate:

"Without a coffin I shall lie
And sleep my sleep eternal—
Not even a shell, my only chance
Of being made a colonel."

We remember the rival lovers going out to fight a duel — how they chose a friend apiece to remind them of the pleasant fact that, even when dead, they would still have two seconds to live; how when they took their places, fear made them tremble so that they found, to their astonishment, they were both shaking hands; how one offered to withdraw his charge against the other if that other's ramrod would do the same; how they nevertheless felt that if they went off without a shot there would be strange reports; and how, when they had aimed, not at one another but at the sun, the chronicler expressed a wish that all other duels might have a similar upshot in the end. We remember the soldier bold, Ben

Battle, who, having lost his legs, was obliged to lay down his arms; whose erstwhile sweetheart cruelly rejected him because, with his wooden legs, he now stood upon such a very different footing; and who finally committed suicide by hanging himself with a clothesrope — thus for the second time enlisting in the line. We remember the poacher whom bad companions egged on to poach; the fat coachman whose back was too broad to be conceived by any narrow mind; and the stone-deaf old lady who bought an ear trumpet, with surprising results, since "the very next day she heard from her husband in Botany Bay." These are samples only — they might be multiplied almost indefinitely. But the best way of illustrating Hood's power with the pun will be to take a single poem and read it in full. I select the highly pathetic ballad of *Faithless Sally Brown.* For one dreadful cockney pun — that about "eyewater" — at which the American reader is likely to be shocked, it may be well that I, as a Cockney, should apologize in advance:

> "Young Ben, he was a nice young man,
>   A carpenter by trade,
> And he fell in love with Sally Brown
>   That was a lady's maid.

"But as they fetch'd a walk one day,
  They met a press-gang crew—
And Sally, she did faint away,
  While Ben, he was brought to.

"The boatswain swore with wicked words
  Enough to shock a saint,
That though she did seem in a fit
  'T was nothing but a feint.

" 'Come girl,' he said, 'hold up your head,
  He'll be as good as me;
For when your swain is in our boat
  A boatswain he will be.'

"So when they'd made their game of her,
  And taken off her elf—
She rous'd, and found she only was
  A-coming to herself.

" 'And is he gone, and is he gone,'
  She cried—and wept outright;
'Then I will to the waterside,
  And see him out of sight.'

"A waterman came up to her:
  'Now, young woman,' said he,
'If you weep on so, you will make
  Eye-water in the sea.'

" 'Alas, they've taken my Beau Ben
  To sail with old Benbow':
And her woe began to run afresh
  As if she'd said, 'Gee woe.'

"Says he,—'They've only taken him
    To the tender-ship, you see.'
'The tender-ship,' cried Sally Brown,
    'What a hardship that must be!

" 'O would I were a mermaid now,
    For then I'd follow him—
But O—I'm not a fish-woman,
    And so I cannot swim.'

"Now Ben had sail'd to many a place
    That's underneath the world;
And in two years the ship came home,
    And all her sails were furl'd.

"But when he call'd on Sally Brown
    To see how she got on—
He found she'd got another Ben
    Whose Christian name was John.

" 'O Sally Brown, O Sally Brown,
    How could you serve me so?
I've met with many a breeze before,
    But never such a blow!'

"Then reading on his 'bacco box,
    He heav'd a heavy sigh,
And then began to eye his pipe,
    And then to pipe his eye.

"And then he tried to sing All's well,
    But could not, though he tried;
His head was turn'd—and so he chew'd
    His pig-tail till he died.

"His death, which happen'd in his berth,
  At forty odd befell;
They went and told the sexton, and
  The sexton toll'd the bell."

Yes; this kind of thing is entirely out of date now, I know. Yet if we can no longer admire the fashion, we can surely still enjoy the cleverness. It is in feats of this sort, then—in feats characterized by an almost boundless prodigality in quibble and equivocation, and at best, as in the marvelous last stanza of the foregoing poem, by absolute perfection of attainment, that Hood is, as I have said, unsurpassed.

But now I must find space to exemplify his humor in another direction. Many of his comic poems are really humorous; that is, they produce their effect not by verbal gymnastics, but by essential absurdity of situation and treatment—by the revelation, in other words, of the fundamental incongruity of things. He writes an *Ode to the Spring*, in which the sentimental fancies of the poets are brought to the touch of hard reality: —"where," he pertinently asks (how pertinently will be understood by every reader who knows anything of the vagaries of the English climate),

"Where's the spring in rheumatic legs,
  Stiff as a table?"

33

He gives us a picture of "Our Village" as painted by "a villager," and very rustic and very unidyllic and very unlike the pictures given by the poets the description is:

"Our village, that's to say, not Miss Mitford's village,
  but our village of Bullock's Smithy,
 Is come into by an avenue of trees, three oak pollards,
  two elders and a withy;
And in the middle there's a green, of about not
  exceeding an acre and a half;
It's common to all, and fed off by nineteen cows, six
  ponies, three horses, five asses, two foals, seven
  pigs, and a calf;
Besides a pond in the middle, as is held by a sort of
  common law lease,
And contains twenty ducks, six drakes, three ganders,
  two dead dogs, four drowned kittens, and twelve
  geese —"

and so on, and so on. But for an extended illustration of this phase of Hood's humor, I cannot perhaps do better than to take the *Parental Ode to my Son, aged three years and five months.* This is, if you will, at bottom a study of the real and the ideal. The poet, in his capacity of doting father, apostrophizes his child, linking poetic image to poetic image. But meanwhile the youngster in the flesh gives cause by his behavior for many domestic asides, which jar somewhat with the high and tender emotion of the address.

"Thou happy, happy elf!
(But stop—first let me wipe away that tear!)
   Thou tiny image of myself—
(My love—he's poking peas into his ear!)
   Thou merry, laughing sprite,
   With spirits feather-light,
   Untouch'd by sorrow, and unsoil'd by sin—
(Good heavens! the child is swallowing a pin!)
   Thou little tricksy Puck,
   With antic toys so funnily bestuck,
   Light as the singing bird that wings the air—
(The door, the door! He'll tumble down the stair)
   Thou darling of thy sire,
   (Why, Jane, he'll set his pinafore afire!)
   Thou imp of mirth and joy,
   In love's dear chain so strong and bright a link,
   Thou idol of thy parents (Drat the boy—
   There goes my ink.)

   "Thou cherub—but of Earth—
Fit playfellow for fays by moonlight pale,
   In harmless sport and mirth—
(That dog will bite him if he pulls its tail)—
Thou human humming bee, extracting honey
From every blossom in the world that blows,
Singing in youth's Elysium ever sunny—
   (Another tumble! that's his precious nose.)
   Thy father's pride and hope
(He'll break the mirror with that skipping rope.)
With pure heart newly stamped from Nature's mint—
   (Where *did* he learn that squint?)
   Thou young domestic dove—
(He'll have that jug off with another shove!)
   Dear nursling of the hymeneal nest
   (Are those torn clothes his best?)

35

Little epitome of man!
(He'll climb upon the table — that's his plan.)
Touch'd with the beauteous tints of dawning life —
  (He's got a knife!)

"Thou pretty opening rose!
(Go to your mother, child, and wipe your nose!)
Balmy and breathing music like the south —
(He nearly brings my heart into my mouth)
Fresh as the morn, and brilliant as its star
(I wish that window had another bar),
Bold as the hawk, yet gentle as the dove! —
  (I tell you what, my love!
I cannot write, unless he's sent above!)"

V

It is to the humorous portions of Hood's
work that, as I have said, his perishable productions almost wholly belong. In passing
from these to his serious poetry we enter upon
a much smaller division; but in this division
nearly everything is good, while much is of
rare excellence.

Delicate fancy, an exquisite refinement of
feeling, and that true thaumaturgic touch
which gives a sudden and illuminating freshness
to even the tritest thought — these are among
the salient characteristics of Hood's higher
poetic mood. In the *Plea for the Midsummer
Fairies*, for instance, we feel that Queen Mab
herself must have been with the gentle dreamer;
we breathe the atmosphere of Shakespeare's

own elfin world; there is no heavy earthly
emphasis to mar the fragile texture of the
verses; the whole vision is so light and filmy
that it seems to have been woven out of moon-
beams and dew.

"And lo! upon my fix'd delighted ken
  Appear'd the loyal Fays.—Some by degrees
Crept from the primrose buds that opened then,
And some from bell-shaped blossoms like the bees.
Some from the dewy meads and rushy leas,
Flew up like chafers when the rustics pass;
Some from the rivers, others from tall trees
Dropp'd like shed blossoms, silent to the grass,
Spirits and elfins small, of every class.

"Peri and Pixy, and quaint Puck the Antic,
  Brought Robin Goodfellow, that merry swain,
And stealthy Mab, queen of old realms romantic,
Came too, from distance, in her tiny wain,
Fresh dripping from a cloud—some bloomy rain,
Then circling the bright Moon, had wash'd her car,
And still bedew'd it with a various stain:
Lastly came Ariel, shooting from a star,
Who bears all fairy embassies afar.

"But Oberon, that night elsewhere exiled,
  Was absent, whether some distemper'd spleen
Kept him and his fair mate unreconciled,
Or warfare with the Gnome (whose race had been
Sometimes obnoxious) kept him from his queen,
And made her now peruse the starry skies
Prophetical, with such an absent mien;
Howbeit, the tears stole often to her eyes,
And oft the Moon was incensed with her sighs."

Yet more completely individual even than such delicate fancy as this, is the somber imagination which pervades so many of Hood's pages—their brooding tenderness, their subtle penetrative melancholy. Here indeed we come into touch with the essential nature of Hood himself. For to him as a poet, no less than to him as a man, life presented itself as, first and last, mainly a tragedy —a tragedy with many comic episodes, but still a tragedy. His humor bubbled up continually to the surface of his thought — bright, tricksy, irrepressible; it flashed and played about many an unpromising theme; but there was always sadness in the depths. For he knew and felt the overwhelming darkness of the human lot; he had himself explored those gloomy recesses of existence — those windings and turnings of its *silva oscura*—in which many a one has missed his way, to stumble like Dante along the downward path to hell; he had heard across the ages, echoed in his own soul, "the sad Vergilian cry, the sense of tears in mortal things." Hence the terrible significance of his *Ode to Melancholy,* which seems to be wrung out of his very heart. "O clasp me, sweet," he cries to his wife, after dwelling on the mutability of all earthly love and beauty:

"O clasp me, sweet, whilst thou art mine,
And do not take my tears amiss,
For tears must flow to wash away
A thought that shows so stern as this!
Forgive, if somewhile I forget
In woe to come the present bliss,
As frighted Proserpine let fall
Her flowers at the sight of Dis.
Even so the dark and bright will kiss;
The sunniest things throw sternest shade;
And there is even a happiness
That makes the heart afraid.
Even the bright extremes of joy
Bring on conclusions of disgust,
Like the sweet blossoms of the May
Whose fragrance ends in must.
O, give her, then, her tribute just,
Her sighs and tears and musings holy;
There is no music in the life
That sounds with idiot laughter solely.
There's not a string attuned to mirth
But has its chord in melancholy."

Other poets have lingered over the pathos of our brief human life, and have reminded us that, as mortals moving in a world of mortality, it is part of our wisdom to seize the fleeting hour, and force it to yield up its joy. It was left for Hood to touch us to the quick by telling us of the happiness "that makes the heart afraid."

Among Hood's serious poems there are several which are known wherever English literature is read at all. I need therefore only

allude to the superb *Dream of Eugene Aram*,
in which the workings of a crime-tortured soul
are laid bare with remorseless power; the
Bridge of Sighs, the wild effect of which is
marvelously enhanced by the headlong pace
and mad jingle of the verse; and that pitiful
appeal on behalf of the starving seamstress
upon which, as we have seen, Hood himself
was willing to stake his title to fame. Only
one poem in our language can be mentioned
in the same breath with *The Song of the
Shirt*—Mrs. Browning's *Cry of the Children*—
and even that, in my judgment, lags a long
way behind. In each case a voice was found
for despair hitherto inarticulate, in each case
those who could not speak for themselves
found one to speak for them with all the elo-
quence of sympathy; and the world was forced
to give heed. It is idle to criticize such works
from the technical side. There they are;
and men and women everywhere have accepted
them as belonging to that class of literature,
every utterance of which is, as it were, a deed.

Partly because of their familiarity, partly
because of their length, I must, a little unwill-
ingly, I confess, pass over the works just
referred to, with these general remarks.
Among briefer poems in which the divine accent
is most clearly heard, I must name, even if

in most cases I can do little more than name,
the delicate little lover's song about the *Time
of Roses;* the splendid ballad of *Fair Inez;*
the *Death Bed* scene, so absolute in its pathos
and simplicity; the great sonnet *Silence,* which
the late William Sharp ranked "among the
twelve finest sonnets in the language"; and
those stanzas of reminiscence, beginning "I
remember, I remember," which, I will venture
to prophesy, will stand secure amid far-reaching
changes of taste, when many a more pretentious effort will have passed into oblivion.
For myself, at least, I am willing to admit
these stanzas have a place in that treasure-
volume which contains the things I should
most regret to lose from the accumulated
wealth of the world's poetry. For this apparently slight and incidental poem deserves,
as it seems to me, to be ranked among our
"possessions forever" by reason of the finality
with which it expresses, through a bit of highly
personal recollection, a well-nigh universal
emotion. Who does not from time to time,
in an hour of quiet self-communion, catch
himself looking wistfully backward into that
dim past whose every detail memory touches
with the glowing colors of romance; who does
not love, at such an hour, to dwell upon the
thoughts of the lost freshness and bloom of

those days when life was so different from all
it has since become, and the promise of it so
bright and golden in comparison with the after-
reality; and who does not understand something of the keen, searching sadness, which
none the less is hardly pain, with which the
recognition of this contrast gradually fills the
contemplative mind? And who, knowing
these things out of his own experience, does
not at once feel that Hood has become for
him the interpreter of this mood of regret and
yearning, speaking to him — as Browning says
it is the poet's special privilege to speak, and
better than he could have done for himself —
his own heart's language?

"I remember, I remember
The house where I was born,
The little window where the sun
Came peeping in at morn.
He never came a wink too soon,
Nor brought too long a day —
But now — I often wish the night
Had borne my soul away!

"I remember, I remember
The roses red and white,
The violets and the lily cups,
Those flowers made of light.
The lilac where the robin built;
And where my brother set
The laburnum on his birthday—
The tree is living yet!

"I remember, I remember
Where I was used to swing,
And thought the air must rush as fresh
To swallows on the wing.
My spirit flew in feathers then
That is so heavy now,
And summer pools could hardly cool
The fever on my brow.

"I remember, I remember
The fir-trees dark and high,
I used to think their slender tops
Were close against the sky —
It was a childish ignorance,
But now, 't is little joy
To know I'm further off from heaven
Than when I was a boy!"

Before leaving this second division of Hood's
work, I have still to speak for a moment of
what, viewed from the purely artistic standpoint, is undoubtedly to be pronounced his
masterpiece — *The Haunted House*. Here
conception and execution are alike beyond
praise: from the opening to the closing line
we are impressed by the writer's complete
mastery of an exceedingly difficult theme.
The poem is called by Hood himself a romance,
but it is not a romance in any ordinary accepta-
tion of the word; nor is it a story. It is just
a splendidly sustained description, wrought
with astonishing imaginative insight and skill,
and in such a manner, with so careful and sure

a hand, that, amid all the accumulations of minute detail, every touch is made to tell. The subject is found in a couple of lines from Wordsworth's *Hart-leap Well*, quoted by Hood as his starting-point or text:

"A jolly place, said he, in times of old,
But something ails it now; the place is curst."

Mystery broods over the poem from the first phrase to the last.

"Some weighty crime, that heaven could not pardon,
A secret curse on that old building hung,
And its deserted garden."

What that curse was, and how it came to fall upon the once stately mansion, Hood does not tell us; it is part of the strange and weird power of the poem that we are left entirely in the dark as to the horrible incident which, in some bygone day, had brought down that "prodigious ban of excommunication" under which, year after year since then, the house has been slowly rotting away. Dread, as of some impalpable thing of terror, thus comes to possess us as we read. We feel the truth of the oft-repeated stanza:

"O'er all there hung a shadow and a fear;
A sense of mystery the spirit daunted,
And said, as plain as whisper in the ear,
The place is haunted!"

What the writer offers to us, then, is simply

an elaborate study of desolation, not done with the broad brush, but by the piling up of separate details; a study so complete, so vivid, so realistic, that the least fanciful reader finally yields himself to the poisonous spell. Stanza by stanza, through the three hundred and fifty-two lines of which the poem is composed, Hood collects and emphasizes every fact and image and symbol of waste and decay; there is none so trivial that it escapes his keen attention, none so seemingly insignificant that he cannot wring from it some fresh and horrible suggestion of doom, and ruin, and utter devastation. From point to point we are led through the scene without—where no human figure evermore stirs among the flowers that have run wild and the weeds that have overgrown the once well tended paths, where the birds build in the porch, while the moping heron stands stiff and motionless over the reedy pool, and the rabbit makes his burrow on the lawn—to the house itself.

> "No dog was on the threshold, great or small;
>   No pigeon on the roof—no household creature—
>   No cat demurely dozing on the wall—
>   Not one domestic feature."

Then, passing through the porch where the wren has built her nest, we enter the strange habitation—a habitation no more.

"O very gloomy is the House of Woe,
   Where tears are falling while the bell is knelling,
   With all the dark solemnities which show
      That Death is in the dwelling.

"O very, very dreary is the room
   Where Love, domestic Love, no longer nestles,
   But, smitten by the common stroke of doom,
      The corpse lies on its trestles!

"But House of Woe, and hearse, and sable pall,
   The narrow home of this departed mortal,
   Ne'er looked so gloomy as that ghostly hall,
      With its deserted portal.

"The centipede along the threshold crept,
   The cobweb hung across in mazy tangle,
   And in its winding sheet the maggot slept
      At every nook and angle.

"The keyhole lodged the earwig and her brood,
   The emmets of the steps had old possession,
   And marched in search of their diurnal food
      In undisturbed procession.

"As undisturb'd as the prehensile cell
   Of moth or maggot, or the spider's tissue,
   For never foot upon that threshold fell,
      To enter, or to issue."

Then we grope through the dark chambers, half stifled by the stagnant air, yet chilled as in a tomb. We pass along the silent corridors in which our footsteps echo with a sharp unearthly distinctness; we climb the dusty

46

stairways where a bat — or something in bat's shape—startles us as it whirls by in the clammy gloom. At length, as by the guidance of fate, we reach the room we dread, yet are compelled by some resistless power to enter. There the death-watch ticks behind the paneled oak, the arras heaves in inexplicable tremor, and the lonely sunbeam that steals in to find fly and midge banished, reveals a bloody hand embroidered on the bed curtain, and a few obscure spots, dumbly eloquent of some monstrous deed, pointing across the floor from bed to door. And again and again, with fearful iteration, and as a fitting close to each separate passage of description, comes the refrain with its hint of intangible horror and vague foreboding and alarm:

> "O'er all there hung a shadow and a fear,
> A sense of mystery the spirit daunted,
> And said as plain as whisper in the ear,
> The place is haunted."

No mere summary and no selected passages would suffice to give any adequate idea of the power of this poem; it must be read, and read through, and read at a sitting. To have written this alone, said Poe—and Poe, we remember, was the author of *The Fall of the House of Usher*—would have secured immortality for any poet of the nineteenth century.

VI

Having now dealt separately with the comic and the serious sides of Hood's genius, I must say something of that exceedingly characteristic part of his work in which the two powers are not merely blended, but fused. Strictly speaking, we are perhaps scarcely justified in treating these poems as a distinct class, since in many productions which we should not hesitate to pronounce simply humorous there is a serious substratum, now small, now quite important; and thus the frontier-line between comic and serio-comic could at no place be very definitely drawn. But in the special works now to be considered, our poet is wholly, intensely, in earnest; he chooses the humorous medium because through it he feels he can most forcibly express his deepest criticism of life; and thus the union of elements is so complete — their interpenetration so absolute — that the result may be fairly called a fresh and independent literary type. Because, moreover, these works are of peculiar interest as revelations of Hood's personality and outlook upon the world, it seems convenient to detach them from the rest of his writings and to regard them by themselves.

43

Of course there is nothing unique in such intimate association between the keenest sense of life's essentially tragic conditions and the richest and most expansive humor. The great humorists of the world have often been the saddest as well as the wisest of men, and the foundations of the deepest laughter lie very close to the perennial sources of tears. What Hood himself told us a little while ago is universally true of all humor which has any lasting hold upon us—there's not a string attuned to mirth but has its chord in melancholy. When we consider Hood's work on this side, then—when we read what for want of a better name we may call his Gruesome Grotesques—we do not claim for these a place apart in literature, though perhaps nowhere else is his individuality of touch more apparent. We simply maintain that in virtue of these productions he deserves to be classed among the really great English masters in a particular and very difficult field of composition, and therefore to take a rank higher than that to which either his wit alone or his poetic faculty alone might be held to entitle him.

Perhaps we can best understand Hood's method in these gruesome grotesques by noting the startling effect with which he will sometimes introduce a verbal quibble or bizarre image even when he is dealing seriously with a serious subject. Every reader of the *Song of the Shirt* will recall an illustration of the unexpected employment of a pun in the very agony of the woman's passion and despair:

"Work — work — work —
In the dull December light!
And work—work—work—
When the weather is warm and bright;
When underneath the eaves
The brooding swallows cling,
As if to show me their sunny backs,
And *twit* me with the spring!"

The last line is a daring experiment in contrast. On the face of it, a pun ought to be disastrous in such a context; yet no one, I think, can fail to feel that its effect is that, not of marring, but of heightening the tragedy of the poem, as Lady Macbeth's frenzied pun is felt to heighten the terror of the scene which follows the murder of Duncan. In *Eugene Aram*, again, the poet plays almost ferociously with a fantastic image when he makes the murderer tell us that grief was his grim chamberlain, and lighted him to bed. But—*pace* Edgar Allan Poe, who does not seem to have grasped the significance of this kind of art—what a fearful force such a touch adds to the narrator's remorse! What a white light it flashes into his mind! How true psychologically that maniacal outburst of morbid fancy!

In these cases, then, we have the grotesque element introduced incidentally. Well, when, instead of this method being occasional, the pun, the bizarre image, the extravagant fancy, the playful innuendo, are habitually employed in the treatment of a serious theme, we have what I have called the gruesome grotesques. Take *Death's Ramble* by way of illustration. Such a subject might well appeal to the somber imagination of a Young or a Blair. But Hood chooses to let his wit play about it, to light it up with quip and fancy, to treat it in the spirit of rollicking and seemingly irresponsible humor, and the consequence is that a ghastly conception grows more ghastly than ever under his hands. Or take, again (the thought of mortality was a persistent one with Hood), his *Death in the Kitchen*—a veritable triumph in its kind. His text is from Trim's discourse in *Tristram Shandy:*—"Are we not here now?" continued the corporal (striking the end of his stick perpendicularly on the floor, so as to give the idea of health and stability) — "and are we not" (dropping his hat upon the ground) "gone — in a moment!" On that hint the poet writes:

51

"Trim, thou art right! 'Tis sure that I,
And all who hear thee, are to die;
 The stoutest lad and wench
Must lose their places at the will
Of Death, and go at last to fill
 The sexton's gloomy trench.

"The dreary grave!—oh, when I think
How close we stand upon the brink,
 My inward spirit groans!
My eyes are filled with dismal dreams
Of coffins, and this kitchen seems
 A charnel full of bones!"

With this by way of introduction, Hood
proceeds to pass in review the various members
of the little world "below stairs," and dwells
on the fact that, healthy and hearty as they
may all appear to be, the reaper who never
ceases reaping will in due course mow them
down in their turn:

"Yes, jovial butler, thou must fail,
As sinks the froth in thine own ale,
 Thy days will soon be done!
Alas! the common hours that strike
Are knells, for life keeps wasting, like
 A cask upon the run.

"Ay, hapless scullion, 'tis thy case,
Life travels at a scouring pace,
 Far swifter than thy hand.
The fast-decaying frame of man
Is but a kettle or a pan
 Time wears away with—sand.

"Thou needst not, mistress cook, be told
The meat to-morrow will be cold
   That now is fresh and hot.
Even thus our flesh will, by and bye,
Be cold as stone.—Cook, thou must die,
   There's death within the pot!

"Susannah, too, my lady's maid,
Thy pretty person once must aid
   To swell the buried swarm.
The glass of fashion thou wilt hold
No more, but grovel in the mould
   That's not the 'mould of form.'

"Yes, Jonathan that drives the coach
He too will feel the fiend's approach,
   The grave will cut him down!
He must in dust and ashes lie,
And wear the churchyard livery—
   Grass green, turned up with brown.

"How frail is our uncertain breath,
The laundress seems full hale, but Death
   Shall her last linen bring.
The groom will die, like all his kind;
And e'en the stable-boy will find
   This life no stable thing!

"Nay, see the household dog—even that
The earth shall take; the very cat
   Will share the common fall;
Although she hold (the proverb saith)
A ninefold life, one single death
   Suffices for them all!

"Cook, butler, Susan, Jonathan;
The girl that scours the pot and pan,

And those that tend the steeds —
All, all shall have another sort
Of service after this — in short,
The one the parson reads!"

Does any one laugh at this sort of grim jesting? Do we not rather realize that it is just by such apparent flippancy in the hands of a master that the sternest facts are driven most ruthlessly home?

Hood's greatest achievement in the line of the grotesque, however — many think, his greatest single achievement altogether — is the marvelous extravaganza entitled *Miss Kilmansegg and her Precious Leg.* A long poem, running to some three thousand lines, yet maintaining its brilliancy and its vitality to the very end, this is perhaps open to criticism on the ground that it is really too clever and makes too great a demand upon the ordinary reader, who finds his own faculties at constant strain in the effort to keep pace with the author's subtlety and rapidity of thought, with the wit that flashes and sparkles on every page, with the extreme allusiveness which marks the poem throughout, and with its sudden turns from sportive fancy to poetic feeling, from poetic feeling to sweeping invective, and from sweeping invective back to sportive fancy. But if the work is one to be grappled with, it is one worth grappling with. Hood describes it as a Golden Legend; and such sub-title is full of caustic meaning. A Golden Legend—yes! but in a transfigured, sordid, latter-day sense—a study of mammon-worship in our modern world. The heroine of the narrative—born into untold wealth—loses one leg in an accident; and by way of substitute for the missing limb has one made, not of vulgar cork or common wood (for such would never suit with the taste of the great heiress), but of the pure, sterling metal, with the goldsmith's mark stamped on the calf.

> "A wooden leg! what; a sort of peg
> For your common Jockeys and Jennies!
> No, no, her mother might worry and beg,
> But nothing could move Miss Kilmansegg!
> She could—she would have a golden leg
> If it cost ten thousand guineas!"

What follows—how the fame of the costly limb goes abroad through society and even penetrates the East End; what wonder it everywhere arouses; what honor it brings her; how proudly she figures with it at a magnificent fancy-dress ball; how a foreign count, inspired by greed, throws himself at her foot (one need n't say which foot) and wins her hand—and her leg; and how presently he does her to death by braining her with the leg itself—

all these things may be read in the proper place. But the fantastic plot—the underlying parable of which is at least as important in our own day as it was in Hood's time—is after all of less account than the incidents and comments which are strung upon it. Nothing in the poem is more wonderful than the way in which the keynote is preserved throughout, and every stanza made to bear upon, and illustrate, the central theme—gold and the power of gold in this new golden age of ours. And at the end, the scattered threads of the all-pervading moral are gathered together and re-emphasized in the tremendous lines of the epilogue:

> "Gold! gold! gold! gold!
> Bright and yellow, hard and cold,
> Molten, graven, hammer'd, roll'd,
> Heavy to get, and light to hold,
> Hoarded, barter'd, bought, and sold,
> Stolen, borrow'd, squander'd, doled,
> Spurn'd by the young, but hugg'd by the old
> To the very verge of the churchyard mould;
> Price of many a crime untold.
> Gold, gold, gold, gold!
> Good or bad a thousand-fold!
> How widely its agencies vary—
> To save—to ruin—to curse—to bless—
> As even its minted coins express,
> Now stamp'd with the image of good Queen Bess,
> And now of a Bloody Mary!"

I have gone through my program, and must now bring my little study of Hood to a close. Exhaustive that study has not been; on the contrary, it has been superficial and slight. But none the less I dare to hope that it may help to interest a reader here and there in one who still endears himself to those who know him well as a man of singularly sympathetic character, a jester whose wholesome laugher is still contagious, and a poet of real excellence and distinction. In these days of rapid and vast production in literature, when even the most industrious of us finds it impossible to read half the new books that he ought to read (or, at any rate, that the reviewers tell him that he ought to read), there is an obvious danger lest much that is good in the literature of the past may be swamped and forgotten. In these circumstances a critic who is inspired by a warm personal feeling for his subject may often do a useful if humble service in redirecting our attention to some favorite author, whose value, as he deems, is commonly overlooked, and whose works are not as well known as they ought to be. For such a purpose, and in such a spirit, I have written here of Tom Hood.

HENRY CAREY, THE AUTHOR OF "SALLY IN OUR ALLEY"

I

I DESCRIBE him in this way, for it seems my best chance of enlisting attention for him, since it is almost entirely on the strength of this one ballad that poor Henry Carey takes his place — so far as he takes any place at all—in the annals of English literature. Yet even this roundabout manner of speaking of him may be deemed extravagant in its implications, for of all those who know the delightful tale of Sally and her 'prentice lover (and who does not?), how many recognize Carey as the author of it? And as for the rest of his fairly voluminous work, with the possible solitary exception of *Chrononhotonthologos,* that is rarely enough put down to his credit, not, as he himself rather petulantly complained, because the critics think it too good to be his, but for an even more humiliating reason—that they do not think of it at all, judging from the contemptuous silence of the historians, we may safely say that Carey is one of the most completely forgotten of all the "forgotten worthies" of our eighteenth-century literature.

I confess that I should like to do something to rescue his name from such oblivion. And why not? This is an age of excursions and alarums in the world of scholarship. The spirit of exploration is abroad. Powerful telescopes sweep the literary firmament, and new stars are revealed which would never be discernible by the naked eye. Erudite theses, appallingly prolix and almost superhumanly dull, are written about obscure people — the obscurer the better — whose sole merit would seem to the uninitiated to be that they are the industrious writers' passport to academic distinction. Critics gain reputation for learning and originality by finding out all sorts of qualities of supreme greatness in poets so very minor that the chances are that you and I have never before heard of them. I should therefore only be sailing with the current if I posed as the "discoverer" of Henry Carey and proceeded to make capital out of his work.

Thus I might turn this little paper into a thesis, into which I should of course be careful to rake every scrap of information pertinent to my subject and, to show my "thoroughness," a great deal having nothing whatever to do with it. Or I might make it a eulogy wherewith to convince the world of its blindness regarding those extraordinary merits of my hero which I alone have been privileged to perceive. But let me be candid. This will be neither thesis nor panegyric, because I do not think Carey really worthy of either. He is not, as I regard him, one of those writers to whom posterity is called upon to make tardy amends for contemporary neglect. There is nothing great about the man or his work. But on the other hand, there is a good deal that is interesting—I mean humanly interesting — about both. Carey is, to say the least of it, quite as worthy of consideration as many another minor poet or dramatist of his time who never fails to get his paragraph of recognition and appraisement from those who discourse of literature in the Age of Anne, while he is habitually passed over without a word. And if this may seem a poor excuse for talking about him, let me add that he played his little part in the literary movements of the early eighteenth century with some success, and that his writings, upon investigation, turn out to have more significance than might have been anticipated, for those, at all events, who care to look at literature in its broadly historical aspects. A few pages may, therefore, quite fittingly be given to his memory.

II

Of Carey's life, though the main outlines are sufficiently clear, few particulars have come down to us. We do not even know the date of his birth, or anything definite about his parentage, though common report made him a natural son of George Savile, the famous first Marquis of Halifax, who died in 1695. This report, which there appears to be no reason to question, is incidentally supported by the reappearance of the putative father's names as those of the poet's son, George Savile Carey, who, it may be of interest to mention in passing, was grandfather of the celebrated actor, Edmund Kean. Carey's mother is said to have been a schoolmistress. We first hear of him in 1713 when, as a very young man, he made a modest enough bow before the reading public with a small volume of *Poems on Several Occasions* under his arm. These poems are neither better nor worse than the average run of such effusions at the time, and we may dismiss them by saying that they are of a kind which no mortal man would now want to read. Poetry, however, as he afterwards urged by way of apology, was only a pastime with him. His real profession was music.

Unfortunately, he seems to have been but poorly equipped for his lifework, since he understood so little of the principles of his art that, according to the trustworthy testimony of an intimate friend, he was never even able to put a bass to one of his own songs. His chances of success were therefore exceedingly circumscribed, and we are hardly surprised to find that his chief employment was in teaching in boarding schools and "among people of middling rank and private families." But while lacking in science, Carey possessed a genuine gift of melody, and a ready power of inventing original and catching airs for his own simple lyrics. His songs and cantatas were very numerous and in their own time enjoyed considerable favor, though they would doubtless be pronounced thin and commonplace now by those whose ears are attuned to, and a good deal spoilt by, the intricacies of the music of to-day.

An even better opening for his talents was, however, furnished by the stage, for which he wrote perhaps less frequently than might have been expected, considering the gratifying reception more than once accorded to his efforts. A volume of his dramatic works, published by subscription in 1743, contains eight pieces, and two others, never reprinted, are mentioned in the bibliographies. With one important exception — that of *Chronon-hotonthologos* — these were all of the class of musical plays—or ballad operas, as they were then called—a species of composition which had grown out of the popular Italian opera and was at the same time a patriotic protest against it. But in most cases, curiously enough, Carey contented himself with writing the libretto, leaving it to others to provide the music for him.

The mystery in which the earlier part of Carey's life remains enshrouded gathers about it again at the close. He died in his house in Great Warner Street, Clerkenwell, on October 4, 1743, suddenly, but whether or not by his own hand remains an unsettled question. If indeed it was a case of suicide, then it must have put a quite unlooked-for tragic end to a career which, though certainly not without its difficulties and discouragements, seems, so far as we can make out, to have been rendered something more than tolerable by a sanguine temperament and general good spirits. In explanation of the supposed desperate act it is alleged by some that Carey really suffered acutely from the envy and malevolence of his professional brethren, to which he makes frequent reference in his prefaces and poems; by others again, that he was in serious financial straits. That his condition at the time was far from flourishing is attested by the fact that his widow and four small children were left, as a newspaper advertisement of a benefit performance at Covent Garden put it, "entirely destitute of any provision." But though Dibdin and Hawkins both give the common story without qualification,[1] it is by no means certain that it is well founded. The contemporary record tells us only that "Carey got out of bed . . . in perfect health, and was soon found dead." How the persistent rumor of his having hanged himself originated, and therefore what may be its value, it is impossible now to determine.

III

In turning from Carey himself to his work it will be natural for us to follow the logician's plan of arguing from the known to the unknown, and to begin with that part of it which still makes its sure appeal to the sympathy of readers.

To reproduce the ballad of *Sally in Our*

[1] Dibdin sums up Carey's life and death in a single pithy sentence which is worth quoting as a curiosity of construction. Carey, he writes, "led a life far from reproach, and hanged himself October 4th, 1743."

Alley, or even to make extracts from it might, in view of its familiarity, be justly deemed a work of supererogation.   But as this is one of those poems which we are all glad of an excuse to read once again, I yield to the temptation and give it here in full.

SALLY IN OUR ALLEY

Of all the girls that are so smart
 There's none like pretty Sally;
She is the darling of my heart,
 And she lives in our alley.
There is no lady in the land
 Is half so sweet as Sally;
She is the darling of my heart;
 And she lives in our alley.

Her father he makes cabbage-nets
 And through the streets does cry 'em;
Her mother she sells laces long
 To such as please to buy 'em:
But sure such folks could ne'er beget
 So sweet a girl as Sally!
She is the darling of my heart;
 And she lives in our alley.

When she is by, I leave my work;
 I love her so sincerely;
My master comes like any Turk;
 And bangs me most severely —
But let him bang his bellyful,
 I 'll bear it all for Sally;
She is the darling of my heart,
 And she lives in our alley.

HENRY CAREY

Of all the days that's in the week
   I dearly love but one day —
And that's the day that comes betwixt
   A Saturday and Monday;
For then I'm drest all in my best
   To walk abroad with Sally;
She is the darling of my heart,
   And she lives in our alley.

My master carries me to church,
   And often am I blamed
Because I leave him in the lurch
   As soon as text is named;
I leave the church in sermon-time
   And slink away to Sally;
She is the darling of my heart,
   And she lives in our alley.

When Christmas comes about again
   O then I shall have money;
I'll hoard it up, and box it all,
   I'll give it to my honey:
I would it were ten thousand pound,
   I'd give it all to Sally;
She is the darling of my heart,
   And she lives in our alley.

My master and the neighbors all
   Make game of me and Sally,
And, but for her, I'd better be
   A slave and row a galley;
But when my seven long years are out
   O then I'll marry Sally, —
O then we'll wed, and then we'll bed . . .
   But not in our alley!

Now I need not consume space in praises of such a little masterpiece as this; it will be enough to quote Mr. Palgrave's remark that it is worthy of the Ancients from its combination of "grace, tenderness, simplicity, and humor," and even more "from the completeness and unity of the picture presented." But as very few, I imagine, of those who have enjoyed it as a ballad have ever been at the trouble to scrutinize its poetic character, consider the circumstances in which it was written, or estimate its significance from the historical point of view, it is at these things that we may properly make it our business to glance.

In a note prefixed to the poem when it was first included in a collection of his verse, Carey has himself given us a most delightful account of its origin. Its purpose was, he declares, "to set forth the Beauty of a chaste and disinterested Passion, even in the lowest Class of Human Life." And he continues: "The real Occasion was this: A Shoemaker's 'Prentice making Holiday with his Sweetheart, treated her with a Sight of Bedlam, the Puppet-shows, the Flying Chairs, and all the Elegancies of Moorfields"—at that period, as ever since the time of Henry II, a popular place of resort for cockney pleasure-seekers. "From whence proceeding to the Farthing

Pye-House, he gave her a Collation of Buns, Cheesecakes, Gammon of Bacon, Stuff'd Beef, and Bottled Ale," a feast which, while it shows that a chaste passion need not interfere with a robust appetite, also suggests the saddening reflection that the digestion of youth must have been stronger then than it is now. "Through all these Scenes," Carey goes on, "the Author dodged them, charmed with the Simplicity of their Courtship: from whence he drew this little Sketch of Nature." But being then young and obscure, he adds, "he was much ridiculed by some of his Acquaintance for this Performance: which nevertheless made its Way into the Polite World, and amply recompensed him by the Applause of the divine Addison, who was pleased (more than once) to mention it with approbation."

These naïve remarks provide an admirable introduction to the ballad which, re-read in the light of them, will be found to gain a freshness of interest in at least two ways. In the first place, the little story purports to be—and we have neither right nor reason to question the author's statement—a direct transcript from real life. This fact should itself deepen its human meaning for us; to me, at any rate, it gives an additional pleasure

to feel behind the shadow-figures of the poet
the substantial flesh-and-blood actuality of
the young shoemaker and his buxom lass.
But this is not now the chief thing to be
considered. The point is, that it is the life
of the "lowest class" of society which furnished the poet with the theme of his idyll.
Sally's father, as we have just read, hawked
cabbage-nets of his own making through the
streets; her mother sold laces to such as
"might please to buy 'em." The lover
himself was only a 'prentice lad whose master
was wont, after the good old fashion of those
days, to "bang" him soundly for idling his
time away in fond oglings after the maiden
who made his heart beat faster whenever
she came in sight.

A strange, uncouth hero and a novel sort
of heroine for a sentimental love poem!
Queer substitutes indeed for the swains and
nymphs, the Corydons and Phylisses, who
in an orthodox pastoral landscape having
little resemblance to the common English
fields, did poetic duty for the simple folk
of the rough workaday world! Such would
be the natural judgment of readers of "good
taste" in that Augustan age when people
were terribly concerned about the "dignity"
of literature, when the theory of the stage

and the practice of the romancers kept all high passion for men and women of the "porcelain clay" of earth, and the critics were beyond all things anxious that the Muse should not smutch her raiment by wandering out of Arcadia into the dirty walks of "low" life. But Carey had found a real idyll where few of his poetic contemporaries would have dreamed of looking for one; he had felt its winning charm, and he set himself to reproduce it as well as he could in his own unsophisticated verse. And though "some of his acquaintance" might deem him a fool for his pains, the sweet, natural note of his song presently arrested the attention of even the artificial and jaded "polite world" of his day. To us, now that literature has long since abandoned her dignity and is willing to deal freely with the romance and beauty somewhere hidden away in every phase of human experience, there may be nothing particularly striking or original in Carey's little "sketch of Nature." We can understand its real importance, therefore, only when by an effort of imagination we put ourselves back for the moment in the period of its composition.

And this real importance will become clearer if we examine the full bearings of

Addison's favorable opinion of Carey's work. Augustan of the Augustans as he was in his literary standards and ideals, that excellent critic—for excellent he was according to his lights—consistently represented the prevailing taste and spirit of his time. In him its so-called classicism found one of its most complete exponents. His own verse, so ridiculously overpraised by Macaulay, is marked by the mechanical correctness which it was held to be the poet's chief excellence to attain. When he turned to the serious business of the stage it was to produce a frigid tragedy in strict adherence to the pseudo-classic model. His famous criticism on *Paradise Lost*, while it did much to bring Milton into favor among eighteenth-century readers, succeeded in this largely by virtue of its limitations, and is mainly of interest to us now as an example of an obsolete method. His feeling, or want of feeling for nature, which he occasionally patronized but on the whole regarded as a very poor substitute for art, and the contempt which he expressed for Gothic architecture, then, along with everything else belonging to the Middle Ages, commonly treated as barbarous, in like manner reveal his close affinity with his time.

Yet there were ways in which Addison

transcended the taste of that time, and one
of these was the genuine interest which he
more than once manifested in a kind of poetry
then almost entirely ignored by cultivated
readers and official critics—the popular ballad
and song. In following the history of the
ballad revival (itself an important phase of
the democratization of literature) during the
latter half of the eighteenth century, we can
hardly throw too much weight upon the earlier
influence of Addison in breaking the ground
and opening the way. It is true that it is
difficult for us now to read without a smile
the pages in which he solemnly and cautiously
sets forth the artistic claims of the popular
ballad — their tone is so apologetic and their
praise so condescending; but we must not
forget that here too, as in the case of Milton,
his advocacy told the more directly because
it was based upon considerations and made
use of arguments which his readers could
readily appreciate.

His most noteworthy effort to gain a hear-
ing for the ancient folk song was his critical
dissertation on *Chevy Chase*, in which his
principal aim was to show that the unknown
maker of that stirring old ballad had actually
followed the "rules" of the classic epic as
faithfully as if "the Stagirite" had "o'er-

looked each line." But even more instructive
for us is his later essay on *The Babes in the
Wood.* Beginning in a vein of light humor
which, pleasant as it is, is clearly dictated
by the characteristic dread of being taken
too seriously, he goes on to describe the
poem as "a plain, simple copy of Nature,
destitute of all the helps and ornaments of
art," yet charming "for no other reason
but because it is a copy of Nature." There is
indeed "a despicable simplicity" in the
verse; the phrasing is "abject," the expression "poor." All this is admitted. But the
sentiments are so "genuine and unaffected,"
the whole narrative has something in it so
"moving," that the poem is certain to touch
the "mind of the most polite reader with
inward meltings of humanity and compassion." Then follows the inevitable reference
to classic authority, and the "polite reader,"
we may surmise, was relieved to know that
if he gave way to his "inward meltings"
and wept over the untoward fate of the
"pretty babes," he might do so with proper
justification, since Horace would have approved his tears. The entire essay is curiously
suggestive of that tendency to "damn with
faint praise" which, according to Pope's
spiteful description, was one of Addison's

characteristics. But taken in the light of history it is seen to be one of the first indications of the breaking up of the great Augustan tradition, and a critical anticipation of the revival in English poetry of the natural note and the simple utterance which had so long been absent from it.

It is now quite evident why the "divine Addison" was so pleasantly impressed by *Sally in Our Alley.* This ballad, too, was part of the revival in poetry of the natural note and the simple utterance. So much Addison saw, and he welcomed it accordingly. But what he did not and of course could not see, as we can realize very clearly, looking back, is that Carey's unpretentious little idyll has an even larger interest in the literary movements of the time. For it is an early manifestation of that rising democratic spirit in literature which was soon to produce the plays of Lillo and the novels of Richardson, and in fullness of time to give birth to the poems of Burns and Cowper, of Crabbe and Wordsworth.

IV

Carey's other poems, though there are several among them which fall into general line with *Sally,* have now relatively little interest for us. An exception may, however, be made in favor of the once well-known lines, *Namby-Pamby, or a Panegyric on the New Versification*, if only for the reason that they added to our vocabulary the useful and expressive compound which forms their principal title. The parody was directed against Ambrose Phillips ("Namby-Pamby," it is hardly necessary to explain, is a jocular diminutive of that gentleman's Christian name), who is remembered chiefly for his friendship with Addison and his quarrel with Pope, but who turns out, as will be seen, to have yet a third claim to distinction. Phillips had gained a certain reputation by the perpetration of sundry "odes" ("odicles" Gray might have called them) in short lines of studied simplicity to or about various aristocratic children of his acquaintance — the address *To Miss Margaret Pulteney (Daughter of Daniel Pulteney, Esq.) in the Nursery*, for example, and that *To Miss Charlotta Pulteney in her Mother's Arms*, and the *Supplication for Miss Carteret, in the Smallpox*. The virtue of these effusions may be inferred from such a specimen as the following:

"Dimply damsel, sweetly smiling,
All caressing, none beguiling,
Bud of beauty, fairly blowing,

Every charm to Nature owing,
This and that new thing admiring,
Much of this and that enquiring—"

and so on, and so on. It will be seen that
Dr. Johnson was scarcely guilty of unreason-
able censoriousness when he remarked, with
characteristic ponderosity, that these poems
"are not loaded with much thought." They
are not. Now Carey liked simplicity; but
this kind of simplicity was puerile and mawkish,
and in a happy moment he strung together a
number of jingling lines which, if rather
coarse in places, cleverly hit off the manner
of his brother bard and raised a laugh against
him. As thus:

"All ye poets of the age!
All ye witlings of the stage!
Learn your jingles to reform,
Crop your numbers and conform;
Let your little verses flow
Gently, sweetly, row by row,
Let the verse the subject fit,
Little subject, little wit,
Namby-Pamby is your guide,
Albion's joy, Hibernia's pride . . .
Now the venal poet sings
Baby clouts and baby things,
Baby dolls and baby houses,
Little misses, little spouses,
Little playthings, little toys,
Little girls and little boys."

Greatly to the poor author's annoyance, this amusing trifle, like *Sally in Our Alley*, was very commonly allowed to pass as the work of this or that other writer. In his epistle on Stage Tyrants he very naturally complains of such unfair treatment; however insignificant his performance may be, a man wants the credit which is his due, and this Carey, for some reason, always found it difficult to obtain.

"Alas! what Fame, what Gain can I propose,
  When others father fast as I compose?
  To such a pitch is pert Presumption grown
  'Tis well if this poor Piece be thought my own.
  So when, long since, in simple Sonnet Lays [!]
  I made the 'Prentice sing his Sally's Praise,
  Tho' rude the Numbers, yet the Subject mov'd,
  Immortal Addison the Song approv'd;
  Then Prejudice with Envy did combine,
  Because 't was good, 't was thought too good for mine.
  So common Fame did various Authors chuse
  To Namby-Pamby, offspring of my Muse;
  Till Pope, who ever prov'd to Truth a Friend,
  With generous Ardor did my Cause defend;
  Trac'd me obscure, and in Distraction's Spite,
  Display'd me in a more conspicuous Light."

Incidentally, we should like to know a good deal more about Pope's chivalrous championship of Carey's pretensions. The reference to his devotion to truth and generosity of feeling certainly throws a flash of new light

78

for us upon the "little Wasp of Twickenham" whom, unfortunately, we are not accustomed to associate with disinterested actions of the kind in question.

V

As a dramatist Carey began his career with the production of several pieces described as "English operas" after "the Italian manner." For this class of play, in which spoken dialogue alternated with solos and duets, a ready audience had been prepared by the vogue which Italian opera was then enjoying on the metropolitan boards.[1] But the English opera was, as I have said, at once an outgrowth from and a protest against this exotic fashion. Addison, who wrote some lively papers on the subject in *The Spectator,* expressed the opinion of an influential part of the public when he said that "our great grandchildren will be very curious to know why their forefathers used to sit together like an audience of foreigners in their own country, and to hear whole plays acted before them in a tongue which they did not understand." Addison himself had tried his hand

[1]The foundations of English opera had indeed been laid at the end of the preceding century by Henry Purcell, but its growth was for a time checked by the popularity of the Italian form. Strictly speaking, therefore, it is its revival to which reference is made in this text.

with a counter-attraction in *Rosamund*, and though this proved a failure, it had opened the way for many other experiments in the same line. Carey's performances (whether, like *Amelia*, serious, or, like *The Honest Yorkshireman*, farcical) may be dismissed as average specimens of their kind.

A later effort of his, however, though of slighter texture, calls for more particular mention. This is the interlude entitled *Nancy, or The Parting Lovers*, originally presented in 1739 on the outbreak of the war with Spain. His own "argument" will show the intimate connection in theme and spirit, and therefore in historical significance, between this little piece and his idyll of the alley. "The subject of this interlude," he wrote at the time of its publication, "is taken from Nature itself, and discovers the Force of Love in Low Life. The Occasion was this. At the Beginning of the late Impress, the Author saw a young Fellow hurried away by a Press-Gang, and followed by his Sweetheart, a very pretty Wench, and perfectly neat, tho' plain in her Dress; her Tears, her Distress, and moving Softness, drew Attention and Compassion from all who beheld her. From this small Hint the Author drew the following Sketch." Once more we

are pleased to recognize in Carey the interpreter of the humanity which is common to
all grades and fashions of life. On perusal,
the interlude, it is true, strikes us now as
crude and flat. Yet it hit the popular feeling
at the time, and under altered names — now
as *The Press Gang*, and now as *True-Blue* —
it was afterwards more than once put on
the stage successfully when war, or the pros-
pect of war, made its revival opportune.

But the satiric spirit was strong in Carey,
and though he was willing to make all the
capital he could out of the vogue of the opera,
he was even more willing to turn the jest
against it. His two burlesques, *The Dragon
of Wantley* and its continuation, *The Drag-
oness*, are full of verve and point, and reproduce with admirable effect all the salient
characteristics of the operatic method and
style. The former, produced at Covent
Garden, on October 26, 1737, enjoyed the
astonishing run of sixty-seven nights; the
latter, though scarcely less clever, suffered
the ill fortune of most sequels and was received with much fainter applause. On the
title page of the printed *Dragon* the author's
name is transformed to "Sig. Carine." In
his dedication to his friend, John Lampe, who
provided the music, Carey wrote over the

same suggestive signature: "Many joyous Hours have we shared during its composition, chopping and changing, lopping, eking out and coining of Words, Syllables and Jingle, to display in English the Beauty of Nonsense, so prevailing in the Italian Operas. This Pleasure," he adds, "has since been transmitted to the Gay, the good-natured and jocular Part of Mankind, who have tasted the Joke and enjoyed the Laugh; while the Morose, the Supercilious, the Asinine [sic], have been fairly taken, so far as to be downright angry." Why even "the Asinine" went to the length of losing their tempers is not exactly clear, but we must suppose that they had their reasons. Lampe seems to have entered heartily into the fun of the thing, and his music — made, Carey tells us, "as grand and pompous as possible" in order to heighten its contrast with the book—had not a little to do with the success of their joint enterprise. Here is a brief extract from the opening scene, which will serve as an illustration of Carey's method. Margery, daughter of Gaffer Gubbins, enters in great agitation with news of the ferocious doings of the Dragon.

"O Father, Father! as our noble Squire
　　Was sate at Breakfast at his Parlor Fire,

With Wife and Children all in a pleasant Tattle,
The Table shook, the Cups began to rattle;
A dismal Noise was heard within the Hall,
Away they flew, the Dragon scar'd them all:
He drank up all their Coffee at a sup;
And next devour'd their Toast and Butter up."

Such gastronomic feats seem to indicate that the Dragon is after all a rather domesticated monster. But his onslaught upon the breakfast table is productive of a general upheaval in the household, as we learn from the aria which follows:

"But to hear the Children mutter
When they lost their Bread and Butter,
    And to see my Lady moan,
    Oh, 'twould melt a Heart of Stone!
Here the Squire with Servants wrangling;
There the Maids and Mistress jangling;
And the pretty hungry Dears
All together by the Ears,
    Scrambling for a Barley-Cake;
    Oh, 'twould make one's Heart to ake."

Carey's burlesque operas owe much of course to Gay's famous "Newgate Pastoral," the *Beggars' Opera;* but he is not to be denied the credit of having done exceedingly well on the lines which his predecessor had opened up.

These parodies bring us round to another of Carey's works, and the one which, leaving

Sally in Our Alley out of the question, has
done most to preserve his name from oblivion.
This (to give it its full title) is *Chronon-*
hotonthologos, the Most Tragical Tragedy
that was ever Tragediz'd by any Company
of Tragedians. Here again Carey did not
strike out for himself. His own "tragedy
of half an act" was produced in 1734; and
it is evident that the impulse to its composition must have been derived directly
from Fielding's *Tragedy of Tragedies, or the*
Life and Death of Tom Thumb the Great,
which was performed with much applause in
1730 (and incidentally, it is said, made Swift
laugh for the only time on record) and ex-
panded from two acts to three the following
year. Fielding (working in his turn on the
inspiration of *The Rehearsal*) had made
terrific havoc among the tragic writers then
in possession of the stage, and shortly afterwards, in his marvelously clever but fear-
fully coarse *Covent Garden Tragedy*, had
pressed home the attack with an elaborate
burlesque of Namby-Pamby Phillips' *Dis-*
tressed Mother. On these hints Carey wrote.
But though to this extent an imitator, he
was by no means a mere imitator, and in its
own way his work is as well conceived and as
deftly wrought as that of his model.

To enjoy *Chrononhotonthologos* to the full it is
of course necessary to have a more intimate
knowledge than most of us to-day can be
expected to possess, of the plays and playwrights of the close of the seventeenth and
first few decades of the eighteenth centuries.
Yet though details may escape us, and some of
the wit may therefore appear rather childish
and unprofitable, it is not difficult to realize
the general scope and drift of Carey's fooling.
All that is requisite for this is to remember
that the English tragedy of the time was
still vitiated by the rant and inflated bom-
bast of the "heroic" type of play, and that
such experiments as were here and there
made in favor of greater restraint and decorum
—as in *Cato* and *The Distressed Mother*—
only offered the most chilling rhetoric as a
substitute for the older extravagance. Carey
saw, and saw rightly, that the contemporary
stage was hopelessly divorced from nature
and reality, and it was against its stilted
conventions, its inane verbiage, its violent
apings of genuine passion, that he directed
his spirited attack.

About a consistent plot he did not trouble
himself. A few incidents, devised to travesty
the prevailing mode, were enough for his purpose. These provided him with the opportunity

he wanted for his burlesque of the fashionable tragic style.

The scene opens in the antechamber of the king. Rigdum-Funnidos inquires of a fellow-courtier after their royal master.

"Aldiborontiphoscophornio,
　Where left you Chrononhotonthologos?"[1]

His Majesty, he learns, is fast asleep,

"Fatigu'd with the tremendous toils of war;
　Within his tent, on downy couch succumbent,
　Himself he unfatigues with gentle slumbers."

One often wakes from a nap in a state of irritability. This is the case with the king, who announces his intention of forthwith banishing Somnus, the god of sleep, from his dominions. He orders that a grand pantomime shall be prepared to "keep all mankind eternally awake." In the midst of the entertainment, however, news is brought that the King of the Antipodes has invaded Queerummania with a mighty army. Chrononhotonthologos, true to his heroic rôle, is not in the least upset. He sends his great captain, Bombardinian, forth to meet the foe, and issues commands for the due celebration of the coming victory.

[1] It may be recalled that Rigdum-Funnidos and Aldiborontiphoscophornio were Scott's nicknames for the Ballantyne brothers.

"Meantime, bid all the priests prepare their temples
  For rites of triumph.   Let the singing singers
  With vocal voices most vociferous,
  In sweet vociferation outvociferize
  Ev'n sound itself."

The King of the Antipodes is taken prisoner, and despite the fact that that monarch walks with his head where his feet should be, the queen, Fadladinida, falls in love with him on the spot. This gives rise to a little complication of interest and to some passages of a sentimental kind between the queen and her favorite attendant, quite in the approved tragic style. A delightful touch is introduced when the queen invites her ladies to take tea with her, and, with a sudden lapse from tragic dignity, remarks:

"Bring in the tea things.   Does the kettle boil?"

A few lines of this commonplace character, cleverly interjected from time to time, serve by contrast to bring out the bombastic quality of the rest of the dialogue.

While the queen's love for the interesting captive is taking its destined course, the king accepts an invitation from Bombardinian to drink wine with him in his tent. Seated at table with the general and two ladies, who are of the party, His Majesty expresses his readiness to eat as well as drink. No sooner said than done, replies Bombardinian, in effect:

"See that the table instantly be spread,
  With all that art and nature can produce,
  Traverse from pole to pole; sail round the globe;
  Bring every eatable that can be eat;
  The king shall eat, though all mankind be starv'd."

This has the genuine grandiose ring of the heroic stage. Unfortunately, the practical cook, who evidently belongs to a much more commonplace world, raises difficulties.

"I am afraid his majesty will be starved before I can run round the world for a dinner. Besides, where's the money?"

Such a question is naturally too much for our tragedy king. He falls into a violent temper, threatens the cook with instant death, and is not in the least appeased when that functionary replies:

"O pray, your majesty, spare my life; there's some nice cold pork in the pantry; I'll hash it up for your majesty in a minute."

The king, without more ado, kills the "audacious slave" for daring to make such a vulgar suggestion. Then follows a quarrel between Chrononhotonthologos and Bombardinian in which the latter receives a blow. The general's outraged feelings burst forth in a speech for which many models could be found on the stage of Carey's time. It admirably satirizes the fustian which was then accepted as sublimity.

"A blow! Shall Bombardinian take a blow?
  Blush, blush, thou sun! Start back, thou rapid ocean!
  Hills, vales, seas, mountains! all commixing crumble,
  And into chaos pulverize the world;
  For Bombardinian has received a blow,
  And Chrononhotonthologos shall die."

A fight ensues, and the king is slain. Then Bombardinian realizes the enormity of his action, and for the moment thinks only of his escape:

          "Ha! What have I done?
  Go, call a coach, and let a coach be call'd,
  And let the man that calls it be the caller;
  And in his calling, let him nothing call
  But coach! coach! coach! Oh, for a coach, ye gods!"

But Bombardinian knows his business as a stage hero, and when the physician arrives in hot haste, he rises to the level of the great occasion.

DOCTOR. My lord, he's far beyond the power of physic;
His soul has left his body and this world.

BOMB. Then go to t'other world and fetch it back
        (*Kills him*)
And if I find thou triflest with me there;
I'll chase thy shade through myriads of orbs,
And drive thee far beyond the verge of nature.
Ha! call'st thou, Chrononhotonthologos?
I come! Your faithful Bombardinian comes!

He comes in worlds unknown to make new wars,
And gain thee empires numerous as the stars.

With which exordium, he completes his duty
by slaying himself. We do not wonder that
those gathered about, witnesses of this thrilling
scene, "all groan a tragedy groan." Nothing
could be more appropriate.

Even to-day, when the absurdities here
caricatured have long since given place on
the stage to others of a different kind, *Chrononhotonthologos* may still be depended upon
to furnish half an hour's genuine amusement.
For one thing in particular Carey deserves
a word of praise. He has resisted the temptation to over-elaboration, and his lively
little piece gains much from its brevity.

In literature, as in life, one has one's likes
and one's dislikes, and it is often a hard
matter to give a rational account of either.
But I think I know how I first came to be
interested in Henry Carey. In part I was
drawn to him by a certain quality of simplicity
and sincerity which I recognized in him, and
which made him a refreshingly human figure
amid the artifices and affectations of his age.
Even more was I attracted by his broad
sympathies and the wholesome democratic
feeling which I found in his work. Here

was a man who at least was not afraid of common life, and did not hesitate to seek his themes for poetry outside the fashionable world of the salon and the drawing room. Such a man should not be altogether forgotten. And if there is that about him which may still make its appeal to us on the purely personal side, it should furthermore be remembered that despite the neglect with which he is generally treated by the critics, he has his place beside writers of greater genius and influence in the literary history of his time. Alike by his one admirable ballad, by his mock Italian operas, and by his burlesque tragedy, he showed himself to be on the side of the movements which were tending silently toward the liberation of literature from its social narrowness and its artistic conventions. And thus he gave both expression and impulse to that new spirit which everywhere in English life and letters began to be felt with constantly increasing distinctness in the half century immediately following his death.

GEORGE LILLO AND "THE LONDON MERCHANT"

I

EARLY in the sweltering summer of 1731 the well-known actor-manager, Theophilus Cibber, who had then recently opened an off-season at Drury Lane, announced as one of his coming attractions an entirely original drama to be called *The Merchant, or the True History of George Barnwell.* The title itself had a novel sound, and the curiosity of jaded London playgoers was at once aroused. Then little by little it leaked out that this was to be a new kind of tragedy altogether. It was, the public learned, a story, not of lofty passion in a world of aristocratic refinement, but of crime in "low life," while its central figure was no strutting king or romantic hero but a mere 'prentice lad who, according to the crude old ballad upon which the play was founded, had robbed his master, murdered his uncle, and paid the penalty of his misdeeds on the gallows. At this "the Town" took offense; such a "Newgate tragedy" upset in advance all their conventional notions of what was decent in drama, and was in fact an open insult to their taste. They condemned, we are told, "the

presumption of the author in hoping to make
them sympathize in the sorrows of any man
beneath the rank of an emperor, king, or
statesman." Cibber, who had accepted *The
Merchant* with alacrity, now began to tremble
a little in his shoes. But he resolved to perse-
vere with his venture, and on the night of the
twenty-second of June the already much-dis-
cussed drama was duly produced. The signs
were not auspicious for the actor-manager's
success, for among the audience were many
young bloods who had come in merrymaking
mood. An enterprising printer, quick to
seize his opportunity, had in the meantime
reproduced the original ballad, and we have
Cibber's authority for the statement, which
none the less smacks a good deal of exaggera-
tion, that "thousands" of copies were bought
up and carried to the theater by "certain witty
and facetious persons" who hoped to get good
sport out of the performance by making a
"ludicrous comparison between the old song
and the new tragedy." But total failure
waited upon their expectations. As the play
proceeded, a marked change became apparent
in the temper of the house. "So forcible and
pathetic were the scenes," Cibber tells us,
"that these merry gentlemen were quite disap-
pointed and ashamed"; nay more, so complete

was the revulsion of feeling that ere long "they were obliged to throw away their ballads and take out their handkerchiefs." The experiment of author and manager was entirely justified, for

> "The pathos of the drama was so deep
> That those who went to scoff remained to weep."

An interesting detail connected with this memorable performance may be added. Pope himself was present at it, and expressed his satisfaction with the piece.

Though the heat of the season was intense, the play held the stage for twenty consecutive nights, while during the following winter it was again "frequently presented to crowded houses, and warmly patronized by merchants and other opulent citizens," who, for reasons which will become clear presently, "much approved its moral tendency." As the phrase afterwards ran, the downfall of George Barnwell, the 'prentice hero, drew more tears than all the rants of Alexander.[1]

Nor was this the sum of the drama's success. Echoes of the sensation caused by it quickly reached the court, with the result that (as we

[1] I have given in the text the title under which the play was originally produced. Shortly afterwards it was published as *The London Merchant, or the History of George Barnwell.* It soon became popularly known, however, as *George Barnwell,* and by this unauthorized name it has passed into history.

learn from the "Monthly Intelligencer" of the *Gentleman's Magazine*, under date July 2, 1731) "the queen sent to the playhouse in Drury Lane for the manuscript" of the play "to peruse it," and this Mr. Wilkes accordingly "carried to Hampton Court." Now Queen Caroline was a woman of literary taste and, as was well known, took in general but little account of the drama, and her interest regarding this particular production was therefore rightly deemed remarkable. Such evidence of royal favor was doubtless very gratifying to all concerned, though, adds Tom Davies in reference to it, "I have not been able to learn whether the author gained any emolument from the queen's curiosity." At any rate, all the members of the royal family at different times "honored" the play "with their appearance," while thanks to the generosity of the management the author in the long run benefited to the tune of several thousand pounds. When a little later *The London Merchant* was published, it was eagerly purchased by a still unsatisfied public, and by 1735 had reached its "fifth genuine edition."

Such, in brief, is the story of the production of a play which, though barely mentioned in our ordinary histories of literature and now remembered only as a vague tradition, has still, as I hope to show, a good many substantial claims upon our attention. But before I turn to the consideration of its literary and social interest I must first give some account of its author and of the drama itself.

II

Of the author, George Lillo, our knowledge is comparatively slight. Such information as we possess regarding him is derived almost entirely from the gossiping and careless Tom Davies,[1] whose own chief authority, according to his own statement, was in turn a partner in trade of the deceased playwright, then living in retirement in Chelsea. It must, however, be added that of this retired partner nothing otherwise is known.

Lillo's father appears to have been a Dutchman who had settled in England and had taken an English wife. He carried on business as a jeweler — the diamond trade of London was then largely in the hands of refugees from the Low Countries — somewhere in the neighborhood of Moorfields, and there the future dramatist was born on February 4, 1693. Springing from a vigorously Protestant stock, he was educated in the principles of dissent, though

[1] In the *Life* prefixed to a collective edition of the dramatist's works, published in 1775.

not, Davies is careful to insist, in those of the "sourer sort." This point is of importance, for it helps us to understand the strong Puritan spirit of his plays, of which I shall have more to say later on. At the same time his youthful environment, however conducive to morality, must have been thoroughly unfavorable to the development of his dramatic proclivities, the growth of which remains a mystery. He was brought up to his father's trade, and in due course set up in business as a jeweler on his own account. But in the meantime— whether through quiet reading in his scanty leisure or through surreptitious visits to that haunt of all things evil, the theater—his taste for the stage had somehow been stimulated, and by and by the London tradesman surprised his friends and, we may surmise, shocked his fellow dissenters, by doubling his part with that of a writer of plays. He had reached the age of thirty-seven, however, before he made his first bid for literary fame, which he did with a worthless and quite uncharacteristic piece called *Sylvia, or the Country Burial.* Notwithstanding its singularly lugubrious title, this was really one of the innumerable brood of "ballad operas" which had sprung up like mushrooms after the enormously successful *Beggar's Opera*

had, according to the epigram of the day,
made Gay (its author) rich and Rich (the
manager) gay. It was performed, says Davies,
"with no very great applause," and soon found
its place in the ever-growing catalogue of forgotten things. But Lillo was not discouraged,
and the next year he offered a very different
kind of work, *The Merchant,* to Theophilus
Cibber, with the results which we have seen.
The success of this experiment naturally
prompted further efforts, and for the few remaining years of his life he wielded a fairly
active pen. In 1734 he wrote a foolish masque,
Britannia and Batavia, on the marriage of
the Princess Royal of England and William,
Prince of Orange, and in 1735 produced *The
Christian Hero,* a tragedy based on the history
of the Albanian chieftain Scanderbeg and his
splendid resistance to the tyranny of the
Turks. "Too useful and solemn" for "the
general taste of an English audience," this was
withdrawn after only four performances. Then
toward the close of the acting season of the
following year came the powerful drama,
Fatal Curiosity, which Fielding produced at
his Little Theatre, and of which the great
novelist afterwards spoke as "a Master-Piece
in its kind and inferior only to Shakespeare's
best Pieces," and as giving its author "a title

to be call'd the best Tragic Poet of his Age."
This was followed in 1738 by *Marina,* an
adaptation of *Pericles,* and in 1739 by *Elmerick, or Justice Triumphant,* for the matter of
which Lillo went back to an episode in Hun-
garian history. But this last play he only
just lived to finish and did not live to see performed, though immediately after his death
it was "acted with success." He died on
September 3, 1739, and was buried in the
vault of Shadwell Church. An unfinished
version of the Elizabethan domestic tragedy,
Arden of Feversham, was found among his
papers.

Despite his activity as an author during the
last nine years of his life, Lillo does not appear
to have neglected his business—a fact which
speaks volumes regarding the practical side
of his character. The tradition that just
before his death he had fallen on evil days,
though popularized immediately afterwards
by a phrase in Hammond's prologue to *Elmerick* describing him as "deprest by want" as
well as "afflicted by disease" (which may well
have been the case), may confidently be dismissed; we have Davies' word for it that he
died "in very easy circumstances, and rather
in affluence than want." This is indeed shown
by the fact that he left considerable property

to his nephew. In connection with this bequest a curious story got about to the effect that he chose the young man as his heir because he had found him "disposed to lend him a sum of money at a time when he thought proper to feign pecuniary distress, in order that he might discover the sincerity of those calling themselves his friends." The story is romantic, and Davies, who seems to have started it, professed to have obtained it from Lillo's mysterious partner in Chelsea. We learn from another source, however, that the nephew was astute enough to suspect the trick, and knew very well what he was about when he "supplied the humorist on his own terms."[1] But as Thomas Campbell very justly pointed out, the whole incident "bears an intrinsic air of improbability. It is not usual for sensible tradesmen to affect being on the verge of bankruptcy; and Lillo's character was that of an uncommonly sensible man."[2]

In personal appearance our dramatist was anything but an Adonis, for he was short, corpulent, and blind in one eye. Yet his aspect, according to Davies, who first saw and talked with him during the rehearsals of *Fatal Curiosity*, was none the less pleasing; he was

---

[1] Boaden's *Memoirs of Mrs. Siddons*, I, 271.
[2] *Specimens of the British Poets*, V, 58.

"plain and simple" in address and in "his manner of conversation . . . modest, affable, and engaging"; while "in his moral conduct, and in the character, generosity, and openness of his temper" he is even said to have resembled his own Thorowgood in *The London Merchant*—a compliment which, though well meant, is somewhat impaired for us by the fact that this same Thorowgood, as we shall presently see, is a prosy and pragmatical bore. But the most important and most impressive account of him is to be found in Fielding's remarkable eulogy, published in *The Champion* only a few months after its subject's death and while *Elmerick* "was acting with deserved applause":

"He had the gentlest and honestest Manners, and, at the same Time, the most friendly and obliging. He had a perfect Knowledge of Human Nature, though his Contempt for all base Means of Application, which are the necessary Steps to great Acquaintance, restrained his Conversation within very narrow Bounds. He had the Spirit of an old Roman, joined to the Innocence of a primitive Christian. He was content with his little State of Life, in which his excellent Temper of Mind gave him an Happiness beyond the Power of Riches; and it was necessary for his Friends to have a sharp Insight into his Want of their Services, as well as good Intentions or Abilities to serve him. In short, he was one of the best of Men, and those who knew him best will most regret his Loss."

Such a whole-hearted panegyric from such a man is sufficient testimony to the sterling qualities of Lillo's character.

III

So much for the author of *The London Merchant* — a person of some importance in his own day, as we can now see, though wholly neglected in ours. Now for the play itself.

The plot is of the simplest, and a very brief summary of it will suffice. George Barnwell is a young apprentice in the employ of a prosperous merchant named Thorowgood, who is paraded before us as an embodiment of all the virtues, but who in fact wearies and irritates us by his oppressive sense of his own goodness and dignity. Barnwell is a "well-made" stripling of eighteen, innocent and bashful, amorous of temperament, and singularly weak in will. His master, however, thinks well of him, uses him in "affairs of consequence," and entrusts him with "considerable sums of money." It is thus that he is unfortunate enough to attract the attention of an iniquitous woman named Millwood, who having herself suffered in early life through the vileness of men, has come to feel a hatred of them intense almost to monomania, and comprehensive enough to embrace the sex as

a whole. At the opening of the play we find
her laying snares to entrap the good-looking
young apprentice, inspired in part by her
pressing need of money and in part by the
malign pleasure which she feels in compassing
the downfall of any man, however insignificant.
The fatuous youth, hopelessly deficient in
knowledge of the world, falls an easy prey to
her enticements, and his subsequent demorali-
zation is rapid and complete. He absents
himself from his employer's house, and though
Thorowgood's gentleness, forbearance, and
words of kindly counsel so stir him to remorse
that there seems a chance that his better
nature may yet reassert itself, the contrition
is only superficial and temporary. He has
tampered with sin, and when temptation
returns, as it soon does, he is powerless to
withstand its onset. Funds are demanded by
his seductress, and they are provided by the
usual methods of theft and the falsification of
accounts. Nor is this the worst. Acting on
the direct command of Millwood, in whose
hands he is now like potter's clay, and whose
avarice is described by her own maid as
"insatiate as the grave," he waylays and
brutally murders his uncle, a "venerable"
gentleman of "large estates and fair character." All this takes place in a couple of days.

He is forthwith arrested, tried, and sentenced to death; and we leave him in his dungeon, as the keeper enters to announce that the officers are in readiness to conduct him to the gallows. Millwood, I may add, also reaps the reward of her wickedness. The only complication in the straightforward action of this simple story is provided by the fact that Thorowgood's only child, Maria, secretly loves Barnwell, who thus, but for his wrongdoing, might have attained the summit of an apprentice' ambition by marrying his master's daughter.[1]

Such in bare outline is the action of our drama — a regular "assize court story," as Wilhelm Schlegel happily called it. It is, in fact, hardly more than a page out of the sordid annals of Newgate, thrown into dramatic

[1] Lillo follows the old ballad (which may be read in Percy's *Reliques of Ancient English Poetry*) pretty closely as far as the murder of the uncle; after which he goes his own way. This point would doubtless have been noticed by the naughty witlings at Drury Lane had they not been obliged, long before the point of divergence was reached, to throw away their ballads and take to their handkerchiefs. It is commonly supposed that the incidents which formed the basis of the story took place in the reign of Elizabeth; and in the first scene of the play we have references to the King of Spain's "vast Armada," "our peerless Elizabeth" and "Walsingham, her wise and faithful secretary." These, however, constitute Lillo's only attempt at historic color. The "manners" of *The London Merchant* are contemporary throughout. The real scene of the tragedy appears to have been Ludlow in Shropshire, where, according to a local historian, writing in 1822, there was a "piece of ground," still bearing the name of "Barnwell's Green," in which "the wretched victim of seduction waited to rob and murder his friend and benefactor" (*History and Antiquities of Ludlow*, p. 201). Lillo's scene is "London and an adjacent village"—tradition says Camberwell.

form, and might therefore conceivably have been written by that friend of Mr. Sneer in Sheridan's *Critic,* whose idea was to "dramatize the penal laws, and make the stage a court of ease to the Old Bailey." Only a public heartily sick of the heroic fustian and decorous insipidities of contemporary tragedy, and therefore ready to welcome any change that even suggested, however remotely, a return to reality and common human nature, could possibly have given their attention, to say nothing of their tears, to such a production. For, let me insist, the foregoing brief sketch does no injustice to Lillo's work, but rather, on the contrary, puts it in the most favorable light. Often enough, to present in this way the mere skeleton of a play is to leave out of consideration the very elements which would go far to explain its success — the grace or power with which a theme, perhaps unattractive or feeble in itself, is handled; the vigor of separate scenes; the vitality of the dialogue; the freshness or convincing truth of the characterization. But *The London Merchant* has none of these redeeming qualities. It is, to speak quite frankly, a most artless concoction, in which a subject certainly not specially hopeful, but of which something effective might have been made by skillful treatment, is so managed as to exhibit all its defects and absurdities. The incidents are put together with hardly a notion of stage effect; the movement of the plot is clumsy; the dialogue is vapid; the personages are mere lay figures. The play is indeed dull, with all the combined dullness of stilted language, mawkish sentiment, and commonplace morality.

Does this criticism seem to be unduly drastic? A few extracts will be enough to show that it does not err on the side of severity.

First, let us take the following dialogue which occurs on the occasion of the apprentice' visit to Millwood's house, whither he has been enticed by the lady's declaration that she has "an affair of importance" on which she wishes to consult him. Here we have a crucial scene—a *scene a faire*, as the French would call it; and this is what Lillo makes of it:

[*Enter Barnwell, bowing very low; Lucy (Millwood's maid) at a distance.*]

MILL. Sir! the surprise and joy—

BARN. Madam!

MILL. This is such a favour—(*advancing*)

BARN. Pardon me, madam—

MILL. So unhoped for—(*still advances; Barnwell salutes her, and retires in confusion*). To see you here —excuse the confusion—

BARN. I fear I am too bold.

MILL. Alas, sir, all my apprehensions proceed from my fears of your thinking me so. Please, sir, to sit.

I am as much at a loss how to receive this honour as I ought, as I am surprised at your goodness in conferring it.

BARN. I thought you had expected me; I promised to come.

MILL. That is the more surprising; few men are such religious observers of their word.

BARN. All who are honest are.

MILL. To one another. But we silly women are seldom thought of consequence enough to gain a place in your remembrance (*laying her hand on his, as if by accident*).

BARN. (*aside.*) Her disorder is so great, she don't perceive she has laid her hand on mine. Heaven, how she trembles! What can this mean?

MILL. The interest I have in all that relates to you (the reason of which you shall know hereafter) excites my curiosity: and, were I sure you would pardon my presumption, I should desire to know your real sentiments on a very particular affair.

BARN. Madam, you may command my poor thoughts on any subject. I have none that I would conceal.

MILL. You'll think me bold.

BARN. No, indeed.

MILL. What, then, are your thoughts of love?

BARN. If you mean the love of women, I have not thought of it at all. My youth and circumstances make such thoughts improper in me yet. But, if you mean the general love we owe to mankind, I think no one has more of it in his temper than myself. I do not know that person in the world, whose happiness I do not wish, and would not promote were it in my power. In an especial manner, I love my uncle and my master; but above all, my friend.

108

MILL. You have a friend, then, whom you love?

BARN. As he does me, sincerely.

MILL. He is, no doubt, often blessed with your company and conversation?

BARN. We live in one house together, and both serve the same worthy merchant.

MILL. Happy, happy youth! Whoe'er thou art, I envy thee, and so must all, who see and know this youth (*aside*). What have I lost by being formed a woman! I hate my sex, myself. Had I been a man, I might perhaps, have been as happy in your friendship, as he who now enjoys it; but as it is—Oh!

BARN. I never observed women before, or this is sure, the most beautiful of her sex (*aside*). You seem disordered, madam; may I know the cause?

MILL. Do not ask me, I can never speak it, whatever is the cause. I wish for things impossible. I would be a servant, bound to the same master as you are, to live in one house with you.

BARN. How strange, and yet how kind, her words and actions are; and the effect they have on me is as strange! I feel desires I never knew before. I must be gone while I have power to go (*aside*). Madam, I humbly take my leave.

And so on, and so on. Could anything conceivably be tamer, more hopelessly undramatic, more supremely ridiculous? One wonders whether to admire the more the maundering idiocy of the infatuated youth, or the clumsy devices with which his seductress, supposed as she is to be a perfect mistress in all the arts of Phryne or Aspasia, contrives to throw her coils about him.

If any human being, listening to such stuff as this, found it necessary to have recourse to his handkerchief, we are almost driven to the supposition that it must have been, not to dry his tears, but to stifle his laughter.

One general consideration will probably occur to every reader of the foregoing interview. The moralist often has occasion to deplore that in depicting vice in the interests of virtue the writer of fiction, in order to make his lesson clear, is apt to paint vice itself in too glowing and seductive colors. Lillo, in whom the didactic tendency was obviously stronger than the dramatic, has certainly not been guilty of this error.

Our next selection is perhaps even worse— or, if worse be impossible, then let us say equally bad in a different way. The scene is in a wood "at some distance from a country seat." We first hear Barnwell soliloquize at great length upon his dreadful situation, and know that he has murder in his mind. Then the uncle enters—the "venerable" gentleman of "large estate and fair character."

UNCLE. If I were superstitious, I should fear some danger lurked unseen, or death were nigh: a heavy melancholy clouds my spirits; my imagination is filled with ghastly forms of dreary graves, and bodies changed by death. . . .

[*Enter Barnwell at a distance*]

O death, thou strange mysterious power, seen every day, yet never understood, but by the incommunicative dead, what art thou? The extensive mind of man, that with a thought circles the earth's vast globe, sinks to the centre, or ascends above the stars; that worlds exotic finds, or thinks it finds, thy thick clouds attempts to pass in vain, lost and bewildered in the horrid gloom: defeated she returns more doubtful than before; of nothing certain, but of labour lost.

[*During this speech, Barnwell sometimes presents the pistol, and draws it back again, at last he drops it, at which his uncle starts, and draws his sword.*]

BARN. Oh, 't is impossible.

UNCLE. A man so near me, armed and masked!

BARN. Nay then; there's no retreat. (*Plucks a poniard from his bosom and stabs him.*)

UNCLE. Oh, I am slain! All gracious heaven, regard the prayer of thy dying servant! Bless, with thy choicest blessings, my dearest nephew; forgive my murderer, and take my fleeting soul to endless mercy.

[*Barnwell throws off his mask, runs to him, and kneeling by him, raises and chafes him.*]

BARN. Expiring saint! Oh, murdered; martyred uncle! Lift up your dying eyes, and view your nephew in your murderer! O do not look so tenderly upon me. Let indignation lighten from your eyes; and blast me ere you die. By heaven, he weeps in pity for my woes. Tears, tears for blood. The murdered in the agonies of death, weeps for his murderer. O, speak your pious purpose; pronounce my pardon, then, and take me with you. He would, but cannot. O why, with such fond affection do you press my murdering hand? What! will you kiss me? (*Kisses his hand; uncle groans and dies.*) Life that hovered on his lips

but till he had sealed my pardon, in that sigh expired.
He's gone for ever, and oh, I follow. (*Swoons away
upon his uncle's dead body.*) Do I still live to press
the suffering bosom of the earth? Do I still breathe,
and taint with my infectious breath the wholesome air?
Let heaven, from its high throne, in justice or in mercy
now look down on that dear murdered saint, and me
the murderer. And, if his vengeance spares, let pity
strike and end my wretched being. Murder, the
worst of crimes; and parricide the worst of murders,
and this, the worst of parricides.

O, may it ever stand alone, accurs'd,
The last of murders, as it is the worst. (*Exit*)

Comment on such drivel as this is clearly
unnecessary, and fortunately so, for it would
be hard to do justice to it. The foregoing
passages, which are given as samples, will
serve their full purpose if, while they afford
just a taste of the dramatic quality of Lillo's
epoch-making play, they also remind us how
essential it is in our present inquiry to keep
resolutely at the historic point of view. Our
first impulse on reading these extracts may
very naturally be to throw the work aside as
too absurdly puerile to have any possible
interest for us. But our impatience will be
checked if we remember that this is the play
which drew crowded and enraptured audiences
night after night, in the hot summer season
of its production, and broke down the preju-
dices of "the Town"; that this is the play

which Queen Caroline sent for and read from the manuscript which "Mr. Wilkes carried to Hampton Court"; that this is the play which ran through five authorized editions within a few years; that, more surprising than all, this is the play which called forth the praise of Pope;[1] which Rousseau picked out for special eulogy;[2] which Diderot compared with the great tragedies of Sophocles and Euripides;[3] which Prévost deemed worthy of detailed analysis;[4] which Marmontel set beside Racine's masterpiece;[5] which Lessing took as a model for one of his own dramas;[6] which Goethe mentioned with respect;[7] of which Schiller spoke with admiration.[8]

Let me before passing on illustrate one specially distressing feature of this extraordinary drama—its tendency to lose itself in barren wastes of endless, flat, unprofitable talk. Here is part of the scene in the fourth act between Thorowgood and Millwood, now brought to bay. It will, I think, be admitted that there is something large and impressive in the conception of Millwood's passionate sex-hatred. Unfortunately, the effective working out of this conception was beyond Lillo's

1 Cibber's *Lives*, V, 339. 2 *Lettre a d'Alembert.* 3 *Entretiens sur Le Fils Naturel.* 4 *Pour et Contre*, Nos. 99, 100, 109. 5 *Poetique francaise*, ii, 147. 6 *Miss Sara Sampson.* *Dichtung und Wahrheit*, Bk. III. 8 Crabbe Robinson's *Diary*, i, 137.

power. In place of the burning language of nature he can give us only noisy declamation. Trueman, Barnwell's fellow-apprentice and friend, who has just secured the woman, declares that not the least of her faults is the abuse of her "uncommon perfections of mind and body."

MILL. If such I had, well may I curse your barbarous sex, who robb'd me of 'em, ere I knew their worth, then left me, too late, to count their value by their loss. Another and another spoiler came; and all my gain was poverty and reproach. My soul disdained, and yet disdains, dependence and contempt. Riches, no matter by what means obtained, I saw secured the worst of men from both; I found it therefore necessary to be rich; and to that end I summoned all my arts. You call 'em wicked; be it so. They were such as my conversation with your sex had furnished me withal.

THOR. Sure, none but the worst of men converse with thee.

MILL. Men of all degrees and all professions I have known, yet found no difference but in their several capacities; all were alike wicked to the utmost of their power. In pride, contention, avarice, cruelty, and revenge, the reverend priesthood were my unerring guides. From suburb-magistrates, who live by ruined reputations, as the unhospitable natives of Cornwall do by shipwrecks, I learned that to charge my innocent neighbours with my crimes was to merit their protection; for to screen the guilty is the less scandalous when many are suspected, and detraction, like darkness and death, blackens all objects and levels all distinction. Such are your venal magistrates, who favour none but such as, by their office, they are sworn to punish. With them, not to be guilty is the worst of crimes; and large fees, privately paid, is every needful virtue.

THOR. Your practice has sufficiently discovered your contempt of laws, both human and divine; no wonder then that you should hate the officers of both.

MILL. I hate you all; I know you, and expect no mercy. Nay, I ask for none; I have done nothing that I am sorry for; I followed my inclinations, and that the best of you does every day. All actions are alike natural and indifferent to man and beast, who devour, or are devoured, as they meet with others weaker or stronger than themselves.

THOR. What a pity it is, a mind so comprehensive, daring, and inquisitive should be a stranger to religion's sweet, but powerful charms.

MILL. I am not fool enough to be an atheist, though I have known enough of men's hypocrisy to make a thousand simple women so. Whatever religion is in itself, as practised by mankind it has caused the evils you say it was designed to cure. War, plague, and famine has (*sic*) not destroyed so many of the human race as this pretended piety has done, and with such barbarous cruelty—as if the only way to honour Heaven were to turn the present world into Hell.

THOR. Truth is truth, though from an enemy and spoke in malice. You bloody, blind, and superstitious bigots, how will you answer this?

MILL. What are your laws, of which you make your boast, but the fool's wisdom and the coward's valour; the instrument and screen of all your villainies, by which you punish in others what you act yourselves, or would have acted, had you been in their circumstances. The judge who condemns the poor man for being a thief, had been a thief himself, had he been

115

poor. Thus you go on deceiving and being deceived,
harassing and plaguing and destroying one another;
but women are your universal prey.

> Women, by whom you are, the source of joy,
> With cruel arts you labour to destroy;
> A thousand ways our ruin you pursue,
> Yet blame in us those arts first taught by you.
> O may from hence each violated maid,
> By flattering, faithless, barbarous man betrayed,
> When robbed of innocence and virgin fame,
> From your destruction raise a nobler name:
> To right their sex's wrongs devote their mind,
> And future Millwoods prove, to plague mankind.

Now it will not be denied that here and there
in Millwood's invective we may detect for
a moment the accent of genuine personal
passion, but for the most part it is drowned
by generalities which, though doubtless they
impressed their first hearers by their boldness,
leave us unmoved because they are entirely
inappropriate to the circumstances. Here we
may note the point of Pope's one qualifying
criticism—that the author of *The London
Merchant* had in a few passages "aimed at a
greater elevation of language than was consistent with the characters and the situation."
This tendency to rhetoric is, however, one of
several characteristics of Lillo's work which
show that while breaking with the conventions
of contemporary tragedy he was still under
its influence.

The didactic obsession, from which he is never free for many pages together, is another fertile source of undramatic verbiage. Nearly everybody in the play moralizes, in season and out of season, even Barnwell, even Millwood, as we have seen; but the chief sinner in this respect is the prodigious Thorowgood, whose pestilential habit it is to bestow his tediousness upon every one who comes in contact with him and to improve every occasion. In the above dialogue with Millwood we have already had a slight sample of his powers. This is how he belectures the inoffensive prig, young Trueman, whose desire for information regarding the financial situation brings down a perfect torrent of instructive platitudes upon his head.

THOR. Your curiosity is laudable, and I gratify it with the greater pleasure, because from thence you may learn how honest merchants, as such, may sometimes contribute to the safety of their country, as they do at all times to its happiness; that if hereafter you should be tempted to any action that has the appearance of vice or meanness in it, upon reflecting upon the dignity of our profession, you may with honest scorn reject whatever is unworthy of it.

THOR. Should Barnwell or I, who have the benefit of your example, by our ill conduct bring any imputation on that honourable name, we must be left without excuse.

THOR. You compliment, young man. (*Trueman bows respectfully.*) Nay, I am not offended. As the name of merchant never degrades the gentleman, so by no means does it exclude him; only take heed not to purchase the character of complaisance at the expense of your sincerity.

Even poor Trueman's "respectful bow" is thus made the text of a sermon on behavior! And when at the close of the scene that admiring subordinate asks his master if he has any "commands" for him, the inevitable moral reflection is tagged to the reply.

THOR. Only to look carefully over the files to see whether there are any tradesmen's bills unpaid, and if there are, to send and discharge 'em. We must not let artificers lose their time, so useful to the public and their families, in unnecessary attendance.

Later on, the same patient listener is favored with another disquisition on the greatnees and dignity of commerce.

"Methinks, I would not have you only learn the method of merchandise, and practise it hereafter merely as a means of getting wealth. 'T will be well worth your pains to study it as a science. See how it is founded in reason and the nature of things; how it has promoted humanity, as it has opened and yet keeps up an intercourse between nations far removed from one another in situation, customs, and religion, promoting arts, industry, peace and plenty; by mutual benefits diffusing mutual love from pole to pole."

Trueman, whom we cannot but regard as a Thorowgood in embryo, is equal to the occasion, and plays up to his mentor in admirable style:

"Something of this I have considered, and hope, by your assistance, to extend my thoughts much farther. I have observed those countries, where trade is promoted and encouraged, do not make discoveries to destroy, but to improve mankind, by love and friendship; to tame the fierce and polish the most savage; to teach them the advantages of honest traffic, by taking from them with their own consent their useless superfluities, and giving them in return what, from their ignorance in manual arts, their situation, or some other accident, they stand in need of."

" 'T is justly observed," replies Thorowgood, and proceeds to elaborate the economic doctrines which his apprentice has expounded:

"The populous East, luxuriant, abounds with glittering gems, bright pearls, aromatic spices, and health-restoring drugs. The late-found Western world glows with unnumbered veins of gold and silver ore. On every climate and on every country Heaven has bestowed some good peculiar to itself. It is the industrious merchant's business to collect the various blessings of each soil and climate, and, with the product of the whole, to enrich his native country.—Well! I have examined your accounts; they are not only just, as I have always found them, but regularly kept and fairly entered. I commend your diligence. Method in business is the surest guide. He who neglects it frequently stumbles, and always wanders perplexed, uncertain, and in danger."

Happily for us, if not for Trueman, our merchant remembers at this point that it is time for him to go to the Exchange, and the edifying interview accordingly comes to an end. I have spoken of Thorowgood as a pompous and pragmatical bore. The reader is now in a position to test for himself the justice of the description.

IV

In fairness to Lillo it must be said, and said emphatically, that *The London Merchant* does not represent him at his best. That he was capable of much greater things is shown by his later tragedy, *Fatal Curiosity*, in which within the space of three very short acts a terrible story of the workings of fate is carried with breathless rapidity to a catastrophe as ghastly in its own way as that of *Oedipus the King*. Of the immense power of this compressed drama there can be no question; we can scarcely wonder that the metropolitan audience before which it was produced "shrunk from the performance," or that Mrs. Inchbald in some critical remarks upon it should warn the reader not to venture upon its perusal unless he possessed "strong nerves" as well as "sound taste." Yet while in every respect immeasurably superior to *The London Merchant* as a piece of art, *Fatal Curiosity* lacks the peculiar interest of its predecessor, which keeps a distinct place in literary history because it marks a deliberate rupture with a long-standing tradition and a bold attempt to initiate a new kind of tragic drama. It is to these matters that we shall turn directly. Meanwhile they will serve to explain why in dealing with Lillo here I chose to ignore absolute values and to take him at a point where, artistically weak, he is strong in historical importance.

It should furthermore be remarked—again in fairness to our author—that though to-day we find *The London Merchant* dismal, prosy, tiresome, and unconvincing, it kept the stage as a popular stock-piece, especially in the provinces, for more than a hundred years after Lillo's death. This fact is sufficient proof of its vitality. Despite the characteristic protest of Charles Lamb, the apprentices of London were regularly treated every Christmas to "the nauseating sermon of George Barnwell";[1] Hone noting that at Christmas, 1819, "the representation of this tragedy was omitted at both the London theatres for the first time."[2] Some of the greatest actors and actresses of the closing decades of the eighteenth and of the early part of the nineteenth centuries, including Charles Kemble and Mrs. Siddons, appeared in it, though it was

[1] *On the Tragedies of Shakespeare.*   [2] *Every Day Book*, December 26.

generally conceded that in assuming the rôle
of Millwood Mrs. Siddons sacrificed something
of her dignity;[1] while strange as it must seem
to those of us who remember him only in
his later years, Sir Henry Irving frequently
performed in the character of Barnwell when
a member of the stock company of the Man-
chester Theatre Royal.

The popularity of *The London Merchant* is
still further exemplified by the fact that its
story presently passed from the stage to
narrative literature. It forms the theme of
a novel in three volumes which was published
in 1796 and dedicated by the author, Thomas
Skinner Surr, to Mrs. Siddons, who had then
recently appeared as Millwood. This was
followed by the *Memoirs of George Barnwell,
the Unhappy Subject of Lillo's celebrated Tragedy;
derived from the most Authentic Sources, and intended for the Perusal and Instruction of the Rising
Generation, by a Descendant of the Barnwell Family*
(1810). Ten years afterwards this prolix chronicle was abridged and appeared as *The Life and
History of George Barnwell.* Whatever may
be the documentary value of these *Memoirs*—
a matter concerning which we may be permitted to have our opinion—they at least

---

[1] Her *Agnes* in *Fatal Curiosity* was, on the other hand, reckoned
one of her "most wonderful exhibitions." (Campbell's *Life of Mrs.
Siddons.*)

possess one advantage over the original tragedy. They contain a minute account of the execution itself, including "the dying groan" heard "by those nearest the fatal spot," and involuntarily "re-echoed by the sympathetic throng"; and even of the subsequent cutting down of the body. Such particulars were naturally calculated to deepen the impression made by the story on "the rising generation"; for whose further edification there was also added "a parallel between Sir Richard Whittington and George Barnwell," the moral of which is of course identical with that conveyed by Hogarth's famous designs of the good and bad apprentices.

Even well on in the nineteenth century, moreover, casual references in general literature prove that George Barnwell was by no means forgotten. The tragedy itself was ridiculed in the *Rejected Addresses,* thus:

"George Barnwell stood at the shop door,
  A customer hoping to find, sir,
  His apron was hanging before,
  But the tail of his coat was behind, sir;
  A lady so painted and smart,
  Cried, Sir, I've exhausted my stock o'late,
  I've got nothing left but a groat;
  Could you give me four penn'orth of chocolate."

Thackeray used the name George de Barnwell, though nothing but the name, in his *Novels*

by Eminent Hands, for his travesty of the
melodramatic criminal romances of Bulwer
Lytton; while for some reason or other the
play seems to have clung to the memory of
Dickens, who makes various references to it
as a piece of literature well known to himself
and his readers. "Never mind George Barnwell," exclaims Sam Weller, during his first
memorable interview with Mr. Pickwick in
the courtyard of the White Hart Inn. "Everybody knows what sort of a case his was,
though it's always been my opinion, mind
you, that the young 'ooman deserved scragging
a precious sight more than he did."[1] Sim
Tappertit's declaration that the execution of
George Barnwell had "cast a stigma" on the
whole body of London 'prentices, will also be recalled.[2] Again, Bailey, the lively young retainer
at Todgers', whose name was supposed to have
been originally Ben, was known to the inmates
of that respectable establishment as Uncle
Ben, "and that again had been corrupted
into Uncle; which, by an easy transition, had
again passed into Barnwell, in memory of the
celebrated relative in that degree who was
shot by his nephew George, while meditating
in his garden at Camberwell."[3] Evidently

[1] *Pickwick Papers*, Chap. X. Sam's words seem to suggest that
Millwood escaped "scragging." If so, his memory was at fault.
[2] *Barnaby Rudge*, Chap. IV. [3] *Martin Chuzzlewit*, Chap. IX.

Jenkins and the rest of them must have been familiar with Barnwell's story, or they would never have worked their way round to such a nickname. Once more our play reappears in connection with Pip's early experiences and the theatrical ambitions of the egregious Mr. Wopsle. One day, Pip records, "as I was loitering along the High Street, looking in disconsolately at the shop windows, and thinking what I would buy if I were a gentleman, who should come out of the bookshop but Mr. Wopsle. Mr. Wopsle had in his hand the affecting tragedy of George Barnwell, in which he had that moment invested sixpence, with a view to heaping every word of it on the head of Pumblechook, with whom he was going to drink tea." Regarding Pip, who was himself a 'prentice at the time, as having been sent specially by Providence to be "read at," he bore him off to "the Pumblechookian parlour," where the hapless youth underwent one of the most dreadful experiences of his life. Though Pip expressly states that he "never assisted at any other representation of George Barnwell," the account which he gives of it shows that at the very end of his life Dickens still remembered vividly every detail of the play.[1]

[1] *Great Expectations*, Chap. XV.

V

But I need not further pursue the fortunes of *The London Merchant* on the boards or in general literature. Our real interest in the play to-day lies in its historical significance, and to this it is time to turn.

I have said that *The London Merchant* represented a deliberate rupture with a long-standing stage tradition and a bold attempt to initiate a new kind of tragic drama. Now, what was this stage tradition which Lillo had the temerity to challenge? It was the tradition that tragedy must of necessity be aristocratic in its theme and characters. What was the new kind of tragic drama that he sought to introduce? It was the Domestic Drama—the drama of middle-class people and ordinary social life.

It will be remembered that when, just before its production, the subject of *The London Merchant* was announced, "the refined part of the Town" took offense, and condemned in advance "the presumption of the author in hoping to make them sympathize in the sorrows of any man beneath the rank of an emperor, king, or statesman." The attitude of "the Town" in this matter is to us of the twentieth century in the last degree unintelligible. In 1731 it was the logical result of certain abstract theories which at the time appeared to have their foundations laid in the very nature of things. These theories must be considered a little closely, or the meaning of Lillo's innovation will never be understood.

According, then, to the doctrine all but universally propounded by critics and accepted by dramatists, alike in England and on the Continent, the distinction between the higher and lower drama—between tragedy and comedy—was at bottom a distinction of social status. The business of comedy was with the "middling" and lower classes. Serious passion and deep emotion were the monopoly of their betters — of the "illustrious" and nobly born. Tragedy, that great supporter of classicism, the French d'Aubignac expressly declared, inheres not in the nature of the catastrophe (to suppose this were a vulgar mistake) but in the rank of the persons. And even Goldsmith, of all people in the world, writing long after the Domestic Drama had begun, reiterates the same view: "If we apply to authority, all the great masters of dramatic art have but one opinion. Their rule is, that as tragedy displays the calamities of the great, so comedy should excite our laughter by ridiculously exhibiting the follies of the lower part of mankind." Tragedy, therefore, was concerned, and concerned only and to the exclusion of all other matters, with the misfortunes of the aristocracy and the "distresses" of the great. The life of the "meaner sort" was allowed no place on boards consecrated to pity and terror, but was to be taken entirely as a topic for merriment, on its comic side.

Put thus in brief, this doctrine will seem to the reader so amazing that he may be inclined to suspect me of exaggerating in the interests of a thesis. In reply I can only assure him that if this were the place to do so, I could fill page after page with passages from recognized authorities which would furnish ample support for the statement made. He would, however, hardly thank me for such a pedantic parade of evidence, and would soon tire of the monotonous repetition of the same principle in slightly varying forms. I will therefore content myself with an epitome.

By the Italian critics of the time of the Renaissance and thence onward, the aristocratic theory of tragedy was proclaimed without a single dissentient voice; tragedy, we are told by them again and again, is the drama of illustrious persons and can admit within its

128

sacred circle only characters who belong to
the highest social ranks. Where Italian hu-
manists led the way it was natural that the
French classicists should follow, and if we
turn to Pellitier or Ronsard, to De Laudun or
Vauquelin de la Fresnay, to Pelet de la Mes-
nardière or, most important of all, to the Abbé
d'Aubignac, it is only to find the same conception reproduced with unvarying uniformity.
Such critics might differ among themselves
on questions of dramatic structure and tech-
nique; but on this matter of the essentially
aristocratic quality of tragedy they were
one.

Even in the later eighteenth century, despite
the stir of thought and the spread of new
ideas in literature no less than in life, many
of the French critics still clung tenaciously
to the ancient formula. Voltaire, strongly
conservative in this as in so many other ways,
stoutly maintained that tragedy requires
characters raised above the common plane;
while in the *Encyclopèdie* itself—that work
which so distinctly marks the incoming of the
modern spirit—Joubert asserted that according
to the signification which is given to the word
(and as he held, properly given) tragedy is
"the imitation of the lives and speech of
heroes, subject by their elevation to passions

and catastrophes, as well as to the manifestation of virtues, of the most illustrious kind." [1]

The German pseudo-classicists—men like
Opitz and Gottsched—merely echoed the
opinions of their French masters without
adding anything of importance to them, and
among them therefore it was taken as an
axiom that tragedy deals with "men who are
conspicuous by their rank, name, and appearance." On the Continent, therefore, the theory
of tragedy now in question was for a long time
part and parcel of the orthodox critical creed.
But what about England? There surely we
might anticipate that the case was different.
Investigation shows, however, that it was not
so very different, after all. In the great age
of the romantic drama Gosson and Stubbes,
Webbe and Harrington and Puttenham, all
asserted in so many words that the great are
the only proper characters for tragedy, while
Jonson specifically included "dignity of persons" among its fundamental requirements.
These writers represent of course only the
more academic taste of their time. But even
in practice — even in the work of Shakespeare
and his contemporaries — the influence of the

---

[1] In modern France the word tragedy is still defined in this heroic
sense, plays of serious interest dealing with ordinary life and non-
illustrious people being called *drames*. According to this technical
distinction, therefore, Ibsen's *Ghosts* is not a tragedy but a *drame*.
But this is a matter of nomenclature only.

aristocratic conception of tragedy still made itself felt. Romantic tragedy in England, it is true, was never so narrowly patrician as the neo-classic tragedy of the Continent — a fact the significance of which will be considered presently; but it habitually confined itself to subjects remote in quality and circumstances from ordinary life; its chief characters were taken for the most part from the ranks of more or less illustrious people, its temper and tone were unmistakably feudal.[1] Then when in the later seventeenth century the English drama, like other kinds of literature, came to be deeply affected by the precepts and example of France, it was natural that the aristocratic view of tragedy should assume a more rigorous form and be more strongly emphasized. "Tragedy, as we know," says Dryden, "is wont to image to us the minds and fortunes of noble persons"; and again, "in tragedy the design is weighty and the persons great." "Tragedy," writes Rymer, "requires not only what is natural but what is great in nature"; the context showing that like Dryden's "noble," "great" is to be taken in the conventional social sense. Tragedy, according to Congreve, "distinguishes itself from vulgar poetry

[1] Of the small group of Elizabethan Domestic Dramas, which form an interesting exception to this general statement, I shall have a word to say later.

by the dignity of its characters." Later
critics carry on the same tale. "The persons
whose actions tragedy would exhibit to us,"
Bishop Hurd asserts, "must be of principal
[that is, princely] rank and dignity." In
George Selby Howard's *Cyclopoedia* tragedy
is defined as "a dramatic poem, representing
some signal action, performed by illustrious
persons, and which frequently has a fatal issue
or end." Goldsmith's opinion has already
been quoted. Even Fielding, who fully sym-
pathized with Lillo's experiment in the drama,
and, as we shall see, gave it the benefit of his
support, none the less accepted the current
academic distinction between tragedy and
comedy, holding that the latter had to do with
"persons of inferior rank, and consequently
of inferior manners."[1] And such long continued to be the view of critics who adhered
to the classic position, one of whom — J. C.
Walker—at the very end of the century praises
the Italians for refusing to abandon the principles they had learned from their masters,
the ancients, who had taught them that "the
tragic muse should always appear clad in
imperial purple."

Clearly, then, we are keeping well within

[1]This is clearly implied in what he says about the serious and
the comic romances in the preface to *Joseph Andrews.*

132

the mark when we insist that both before and after Lillo's time the aristocratic theory of tragedy was deeply rooted and widespread. Upon what considerations was that theory supposed to rest? By what reasonings was it upheld? Well, in the first place there was of course the inevitable reference to the authority of the classics, and especially of Aristotle, a passage in whose *Poetics* (in fact, mistranslated and misinterpreted) was regarded as providing all the critical ground required. But more important than this, there was also an appeal to experience. It was solemnly contended that the impressiveness of tragedy, and with this its moral power, ultimately depend upon the rank and dignity of the characters; that, in other words, we are moved and influenced by a representation of the misfortunes of the great, while the distresses of people in our own walk of life leave us cold and indifferent. To us to-day, fresh from the perusal, let us say, of *Ghosts* or *Rosmersholm,* such an argument in support of the aristocratic theory of tragedy seems even more monstrous than the theory itself; our one simple and sufficient answer to it is, that obviously it has no basis in fact. Yet in the large literature of the discussion we find it cropping up again and again, and so potent was its sway that those who defended the Domestic Drama were bound to take cognizance of it: among them Lillo himself, as we shall see directly. I will not burden my pages with quotations, though they lie at hand in embarrassing profusion. It will be enough to say that even the author of *The Vicar of Wakefield,* from whom surely a saner judgment might have been expected, lays it down as a rule "having the strongest foundations in nature" that "the distresses of the mean by no means affect us so strongly as the calamities of the great." If this astounding statement has any significance at all, then it is evident that we have no right to take any interest in the "distresses" of dear Dr. Primrose and his family.

The point of Lillo's experiment is now apparent, and the resentment of "the refined part of the Town" fully explained. *The London Merchant* is a deliberate attempt to break down the narrow limitations of tragedy —to make it more human and to widen its appeal by bringing it into touch with the common realities and interests of ordinary life.[1]

---

[1] It may be noted in passing that Lillo's movement toward realism in the higher drama was accompanied by a change in form; prose, as nearer the language of nature, being substituted for verse. This too met with critical opposition. Voltaire, for instance, pronounced prose in tragedy "the abomination of desolation in the temple of the muses."

A few extracts from Lillo's dedication of his play to Sir John Eyles, Member of Parliament for the City of London, will serve to bring out his own view of his innovation. Read without reference to the critical doctrines which I have summarized, much of his apology would seem to us to be in the air. But we are now in a position to see that he is really dealing with issues which, though dead to-day, were living issues at his time. The importance of this dedication as a document will justify the length of the quotation.

"If Tragick Poetry be, as Mr. Dryden has somewhere said, the most excellent and useful kind of writing, the more extensively useful the moral of any tragedy is, the more excellent that piece must be of its kind.

"I hope I shall not be thought to insinuate that this, to which I have presumed to prefix your name, is such; that depends on its fitness to answer the end of tragedy, the exciting of the passions, in order to the correcting of such of them as are criminal, either in their nature or through their excess. . . .

"What I wou'd infer is this, I think, evident truth; that tragedy in so far from losing its dignity, by being accommodated to the circumstances of the generality of mankind, that it is more truly august in proportion to the extent of its influence, and the numbers that are properly affected by it. As it is more truly great to be the instrument of good to many, than to a very small part of that number.

"If Princes, etc., were alone liable to misfortunes, arising from vice or weakness in themselves or others,

135

there wou'd be good reason for confining the characters in tragedy to those of superior rank; but, since the contrary is evident, nothing can be more reasonable than to proportion the remedy to the disease.

"I am far from denying that tragedies, founded on any instructive or extraordinary events in history, or a well-invented fable, where the persons introduced are of the highest rank, are without their use, even to the bulk of the audience. The strong contrast between a *Tamerlane* and a *Bajazet* may have its weight with an unsteady people and contribute to the fixing of them in the interest of a Prince of the character of the former, when, thro' their own levity, or the arts of designing men, they are render'd factious or uneasy, tho' they have the highest reason to be satisfied. The sentiments and example of a *Cato* may inspire his spectators with a just sense of the value of liberty, when they see that honest patriot prefer death to an obligation to a tyrant, who wou'd sacrifice the constitution of his country, and the liberties of mankind, to his ambition or revenge.[1] I have attempted indeed to enlarge the province of the graver kind of poetry, and should be glad to see it carried on by some abler hand. Plays founded on moral tales in private life may be of admirable use, by carrying conviction to the mind with such irresistible force as to engage all the faculties and powers of the soul in the cause of virtue, by stifling vice in its first principles. They who imagine this to be too much to be attributed to tragedy, must be strangers to the energy of that noble species of poetry."

With equal clearness, though in a somewhat more apologetic strain, these fundamental

[1] As several passages in his plays further attest, Lillo's politics were those of the nonconformists of his time.

conceptions of tragedy and its objects are brought out in the prologue to the same play, spoken by Theophilus Cibber, and presumably the work of Lillo himself:

"The Tragic Muse, sublime, delights to show
   Princes distrest, and scenes of royal woe;
   In awful pomp, majestic, to relate
   The fall of nations, or some hero's fate;
   That sceptred chiefs may by example know
   The strange vicissitudes of things below:
   What dangers on security attend;
   How pride and cruelty in ruin end;
   Hence Providence supreme to know, and own
   Humanity adds glory to a throne . . .
   Forgive us then, if we attempt to show,
   In artless strains a tale of private woe.
   A London 'Prentice ruin'd is our theme;
   Drawn from the fam'd old song that bears his name.
   We hope your taste is not so high to scorn
   A moral tale, esteem'd ere you were born;
   Which, for a century of rolling years,
   Has fill'd a thousand thousand eyes with tears.
   If thoughtless youth to warn, and shame the age
   From vice destructive well becomes the stage:
   If this example innocence secure,
   Prevent our guilt, or by reflection cure:
   If Millwood's dreadful guilt and sad despair
   Commend the virtue of the good and fair:
   Tho' art be wanting, and our numbers fail,
   Indulge the attempt in justice to the tale."

Once more the same note is struck, but struck with a much more vigorous hand, in the prologue to *Fatal Curiosity,* which, like *The London Merchant,* is a tragedy of private life, though in blank verse. This prologue is specially interesting because it was provided by Fielding, and expresses the great novelist's sympathy with the democratic principles underlying Lillo's work.

> "No fustian hero rages here to-night;
> No armies fall, to fix a tyrant's right;
> From lower life we draw our scene's distress —
> Let not your equals move your pity less!
> Virtue distrest in humble state support;
> Nor think, she never lives without a court![1]
> Tho' to our scenes no royal robes belong,
> And tho' our little stage as yet be young,
> Throw both your scorn and prejudice aside;
> Let us with favour not contempt be tried.
> Thro' the first acts a kind attention lend;
> The growing scene shall force you to attend."

Here then we have the principles of Domestic Tragedy as conceived by those who sought to vindicate its claims to critical recognition, and to make a place for it on the stage side by side with the aristocratic tragedy of the time. Much of Lillo's reasoning reappears, amplified and elaborated, among the stock arguments of the later defenders of the new type of drama both in England and in France. But this is a matter which need not detain us here.

[1] A palpable hit, in Fielding's best style.

Meanwhile it will be well to remark that the aristocratic theory, though badly shaken, was (as indeed we have already seen) by no means destroyed, and that while the reception accorded to *The London Merchant* was proof of the existence of a public ready for such a play, "the refined part of the Town" still had their misgivings in regard to its propriety. There is a lively scene in Sarah Fielding's *David Simple* which gives us a glimpse both of the kind of interest which Lillo's experiments had aroused and of the position of those who, priding themselves upon being people of taste and culture, translated the theories of the conservative critics into more colloquial forms of speech. One lady in a select party remarks that she actually knows people who had sat with dry eyes through a performance of *Cato* (the feat does not seem to be an impossibility) and yet had shed tears at *George Barnwell*. "Oh, intolerable!" exclaim a number of ladies in chorus. "Cry for an odious Apprentice Boy, who murdered his uncle at the instigation of a common woman, and yet be unmoved when even Cato bled for his country!" Upon this an old lady says: "That is no wonder, I assure you, ladies, for I once heard my Lady Know-all positively affirm *George Barnwell* to be one of the best things ever wrote; for

that Nature is Nature in whatever station it
is placed, and that she could be as much
affected with the distresses of a man in low
life, as if he was a Lord or a Duke." The
significance of this revolutionary declaration —
in which we have of course the expression of
Sarah Fielding's own opinion — is unmistakable; it contains indeed in a nutshell the whole
theory of the new drama on the social side.
What follows shows that Lillo was by no means
without his admirers even among the devotees
of society. For another member of the party
announces that "Lady Know-all and Lady
Truewit have taken a fancy to set up the
author of *George Barnwell* for a writer, tho'
certainly he writes the worst language in the
world. There is a little thing of his called
The Fatal Curiosity which, for my part, I
know not what to make of, and they run about
crying it up as if Shakespeare himself might
have wrote it. Certainly, that fellow must be
something very low, for his distresses always
arise from poverty; and then he brings his
wicked wretches, who are to be tempted by
money to some monstrous action, which he
would have his audience pity them for."

It is evident that the enormous power of
that one single monosyllable, "low"—which
was later, according to Goldsmith, to play

havoc with humor on our stage — had already been discovered by those who opposed the new tragedy. In the light of this fact the social and literary importance of Lillo's break with aristocratic convention in the drama becomes even more apparent. By his innovation he precipitated a controversy which forced upon public attention the long-accepted traditions of the serious drama, and thus ranged in two hostile camps those who abused the new tragedy because it ventured to substitute an "odious Apprentice Boy" for the divine Cato and sought its "distresses" in ordinary poverty and crime, and those who were bold enough to maintain that "Nature is Nature in whatever state it is placed," and that we may properly be as much affected by the calamities of a man in low life as by those of a lord or a duke.

VI

We must be careful to put Lillo into his proper historical perspective. No one, it seems, is ever quite the first to do anything in this world, and though he may justly be regarded as the father of Domestic Tragedy, he had his predecessors in that field. Already in the days of the Elizabethan drama we find a small group of tragedies—surviving specimens

of a much larger number — the substance of
which is provided not by historical or romantic
incidents but by tales of crime in private life.
Two of these crude and violent murder-plays—
Arden of Feversham and *A Yorkshire Tragedy*
—have derived a certain factitious interest
from the fact that they have at times been
ascribed (though without the slightest reason)
to Shakespeare; while the former is also connected with our own author, since, as I have
noted, he left behind him at his death an unfinished adaptation of it. But while these so-
called Domestic Dramas are indeed domestic
in the sense that they deal with homely materials and characters taken from the middle
and lower classes, they have really very little
in common with Lillo's work. Luridly sensa-
tional in quality and coarsely realistic in
method, they represent only an accidental
development of the Elizabethan Chronicle
Play and the Tragedy of Blood, and they
depended for their popularity upon their
success in appealing to that kind of taste for
the horrible which now finds its satisfaction
in the literature of the police courts. No
theory was behind them, and certainly no
moral purpose was held in view. Only one
play of our romantic age really deserves recognition as a Domestic Tragedy in the later sense

of the term, and that is Thomas Heywood's *A Woman Killed with Kindness,* and save perhaps for a passing phrase in the prologue— "Look for no glorious state, our Muse is bent upon a barren subject"—there is nothing even in this to show that the author was conscious of writing a drama essentially different from that romantic kind which then held almost undisputed possession of the stage.

I have said that after the Restoration the aristocratic conception of tragedy was more rigorously formulated and more strongly emphasized. It is significant therefore that the protest against it now became more distinct, and that with this protest the guiding influence of a set purpose also began to emerge. This is shown in certain works of three playwrights —Otway, Southern, and Rowe—who demand attention as Lillo's immediate forerunners, and whose importance as pioneers Lillo himself indeed recognized, for in a passage, which I have omitted, in the prologue of *The London Merchant* he specifically records the fact that they had ventured to show the tragic muse in "a humbler dress." In Otway's *Orphan* for example, we have, as Johnson put it, "a domestic tragedy drawn from middle life"— though as the two principal male characters are twin sons of a Bohemian nobleman, the phrase "middle life" must be taken in a very broad sense. The domestic quality is even more marked in "honest" Tom Southern's *Fatal Marriage, or the Innocent Adultery,* a play which, dealing with a story of the familiar Enoch Arden type, was long popular on the stage and, as readers of *The Rivals* will remember, was one of the books hurriedly hidden by Miss Lydia Languish on the approach of Sir Anthony Absolute. Even more again may Rowe's *Fair Penitent* be taken as a landmark in our history, for in the prologue to it the very principles are enunciated upon which, thirty-six years later, Lillo himself was to lay stress:

"Long has the fate of Kings and Empires been
The common business of the Tragic Scene.
As if Misfortune made the Throne his seat,
And none could be unhappy but the great . . .
Stories like these with wonder we may hear;
But far remote and in a higher sphere,
We ne'er can pity what we ne'er can share . . .
Therefore an humbler theme our author chose,
A melancholy tale of private woes;
No Princes here lost Royalty bemoan;
But you shall meet with sorrows like your own."

As a document in the history of Domestic Tragedy, this passage has an interest which it would not be easy to exaggerate.

But while the plays just named have

undeniable importance as marking the beginnings of the movement against the narrow
post-Restoration theory of tragedy, still more
importance attaches from our point of view
to a little-known work entitled *The Fatal
Extravagance,* which was acted and published
under the name of one James Mitchell,
though it seems certain that the irrepressible
Aaron Hill had a very large share in its composition. In this drama, which first appeared
in 1720 (the South Sea Bubble year) in one
act, and was afterwards "improved into five
acts," and the plot of which is taken directly
from *A Yorkshire Tragedy,* a vigorous attack
is made upon the passion for gaming which
then "raged furiously" in all classes of English
society. More interesting, however, than the
author's ethical purpose is his avowed effort
to make a tragedy out of "private sorrows."
In the prologue, which is admittedly from the
pen of Hill, this feature is boldly thrust to the
front:

"The Rants of ruin'd Kings, of Mighty Name,
For pompous Misery, small Compassion claim.
Empires o'erturned, and Heroes held in Chains,
Alarm the Mind, but give the Heart no Pains.
To Ills remote from our Domestic Fears,
We lend our Wonder, but withhold our Tears.
Not so when, from such Passion, as we own,
Some Favourite Folly's dreadful Fate is shown;

There the Soul bleeds for what it feels within;
And conscious Pity shakes at suffering Sin."

In these lines, as will be noted, opposition to the aristocratic theory of tragedy is not merely conscious; it has become aggressive.

The foregoing rapid sketch, though necessarily wanting in details, is still complete enough to enable us to put Lillo into his proper place in the history of the Domestic Drama. Though as a didactic tragedy of private life *The London Merchant* was not an entirely new thing, its significance as an innovation— fully recognized, as we have seen, at the time of its production—is not therefore to be questioned. As Brunetière admirably said in reference to another matter: "Let us be on our guard against those who are described as precursors; *ideas* in the history of literature, as elsewhere, belong to those who have developed their consequences, and to no one else." This principle may be applied to Lillo. It was he who elaborated and defined the fundamental conception of the new drama. He also pushed that conception to its logical issue. In the tragedies of his immediate predecessors, though the rank of the persons was lowered, there was little change in the nature of the subjects employed or in the feelings invoked; the plots, while involving private interests only, were still woven out of romantic materials. In the story of George Barnwell's temptation and downfall Lillo made capital out of a fresh kind of theme, and produced a play which was realistic in the most commonplace sense of the term. Moreover, in respect even of the rank of the persons his work was notably radical; for it was he who first ventured "to descend so low as to introduce the character of a merchant and his clerk into a tragedy." He put the moral element of tragedy in the foreground of his enterprise, and by his emphasis upon the ordinary everyday virtues of decency, honesty, and thrift broke entirely with the aristocratic traditions of gallantry and chivalry on the stage. Finally, on the side of form, he made an experiment to which not one of his forerunners had dared to set his hand; for while one and all these had adhered to verse as the only proper medium for tragic emotion, he adopted prose for the purpose of bringing the domestic interest of his drama into closer harmony with the actual life it was intended to reflect.

VII

One other aspect of our subject remains to be considered. The appearance of Domestic Tragedy has something more than a merely literary interest. Like a straw on the stream, it indicated the force and direction of a new current in English society. This point has already been implied, but it is important enough to merit a little further attention.

Writing of Richardson's *Pamela* — a work which in the history of prose fiction occupies an analogous position to that of *The London Merchant* in the history of the drama — Lord Morley many years ago laid stress on the social significance of that epoch-making book and of the literary form — the modern novel — of which it is the first true example. "It was not mere accident that the modern novel had its origin in England. The novel as we understand it depends on the interest of the private life of ordinary men and women. But this interest was only possible on condition that the feudal and aristocratic spirit" — the spirit of which Heroic Tragedy and the Heroic Romance alike had been expressions — "had received its death-blow, and it was only in England that such a revolution had taken place, even partially. It was only in England as yet that the middle classes had acquired such a position of consideration, equality, and independence. . . . It was to be expected that the first country where princes and princesses were shorn of their divinity and made creatures of an act of parliament, would also

148

be the country where the imagination would be most likely to seek for serious passion, realistic interest, and all the material for pathos and tragedy in the private lives of common individuals. . . . It was the landmark of a great social no less than a great literary transition when all England went mad with enthusiasm over the trials, the virtues, the triumphs of a rustic lady's maid."[1] This is admirably put; and as I myself have further said in reference to the same matter, if the place of the appearance of the modern novel was not accidental, neither was the moment of its appearance, for "it arose at a time when under Sir Robert Walpole's firm rule England was settling down after a long period of military excitement, and when, with the consequent growth of commerce and industry, the prestige of the old feudal nobility was on the wane, and the middle classes were increasing steadily in social and political power."[2]

Now it is evident that these considerations regarding the novel apply with equal cogency to the Domestic Drama, and that what Lord Morley has said about *Pamela* may quite as truly be said about *The London Merchant.* The forces behind the one movement were also

---

[1] *Diderot and the Encyclopoedists.*
[2] *Outline History of English Literature,* p. 177.

behind the other. "It was the landmark of a great social no less than a great literary transition" when audiences nightly packed the theater in Drury Lane to weep over the downfall of "an odious Apprentice Boy." Like the novel, and for precisely the same reasons, Domestic Tragedy first took definite shape in England. And as an interesting detail it will be noticed that the two forms arose practically together, Lillo's experiment in the drama actually preceding Richardson's in prose fiction by only eight years.

Let me dwell for a moment upon the fact that while the old aristocratic conception of tragedy was on the face of it a matter of literary theory only, it really rested on social foundations. The distinction between tragedy and comedy on the stage was simply one indirect result of those accepted class distinctions which formed part of the accepted order. If all higher passion in the drama was limited to the "distresses" of the great, while the life of ordinary private people was treated as if it could have a comic complexion only, the basis of this curiously narrow view is to be sought in something deeper than artistic convention or academic rule. The practice of the stage followed inevitably upon the caste system which had been transmitted from feudal times and upon its accompanying sentiments and ideals. The drama held the mirror up to nature, as nature was then understood. In the mimic world of the theater the "middling" and lower classes had to be kept in their proper places because they had to be kept in their proper places in the actual world outside. The dramatic monopoly of all serious interest by the privileged few was at once a consequence and a symbol of their long unchallenged supremacy in the community at large.

Here, then, we have the explanation of an important fact to which passing allusion has already been made. English tragedy was never so severely aristocratic as the tragedy of France. Why not? It was not simply because the English drama was less affected by the doctrinaire conventions of classicism. It was at bottom because in England the classes were not so rigorously divided as was the case on the Continent.

Naturally enough, the larger social bearings of their literary theories were but seldom realized by the critics of the time. Now and then, however, we come upon a chance phrase or two in their writings which show that such larger bearings were not altogether absent from their minds. Thus the egregious Rymer lays down the proposition that tragedy requires "such thoughts as quality and court education might inspire"—the court, let us say, of Charles II as an example—and solemnly discusses the question "who and who may kill one another with decency in a tragedy? His answer is supremely ludicrous—as we might anticipate from "the worst critic that ever lived"—but it is none the less very much to the point, for it practically reproduces the mediaeval rule of *quia conditiones impares:* "If I mistake not, in poetry no woman is to kill a man, except her quality gives her the advantage above him; nor is a servant to kill his master; nor a private man, much less a subject, to kill a king, nor the contrary. Poetical decency will not suffer death to be dealt to each other by such persons, whom the laws of duel allow not to enter the lists together."[1] In this extraordinary version of the dramatic proprieties the connection between social code and literary theory is very clear. Well on in the eighteenth century Bishop Hurd reveals his sense of the same connection in protesting against the subjection of the aristocracy to humorous treatment on the stage: "The higher characters being rarely seen or

[1] It will be remembered that in *Humphry Clinker* a nobleman refuses to fight a duel with a squire on the score of their social inequality.

contemplated by the people but with reverence, hence it is that in fact the representation of high life cannot without offence to probability be made ridiculous, or consequently be admitted to comedy under this view."

The rise of Domestic Tragedy then is to be interpreted as one sign of that social transformation which went on slowly but steadily in England from the time of the Revolution of 1688 onward, and in particular of the continual growth of the middle classes in power and prestige. From this point of view two or three features of *The London Merchant* are specially worthy of attention.

In the first place, there is the character of the merchant himself. The growth of the middle classes in power and prestige was in large measure due to the expansion of commerce and its increasing importance to the realm, and as a result, those who were the representatives and custodians of English mercantile interests began more and more to realize their social rôle and political influence. Thus we have the portentous Thorowgood walking the stage in all the full-blown self-conscious dignity of an English merchant, and expatiating in pompous periods on the greatness and utility of the class to which he is proud to belong, and on the benefits which it confers upon the world. Already such ideas had found expression in popular literature. In a remarkable paper in *The Spectator* Addison had described himself standing on the steps of the Royal Exchange, and had told his readers how the "grand scene of business" beneath him had set him speculating on the way in which, while engaged in their own private affairs, the "masters of commerce" were linking the most distant parts of the world together by "bonds of a common interest," distributing "the gifts of nature," finding "work for the poor," and adding "wealth to the rich and magnificence to the great." Steele's account in another *Spectator* of the debate at the Club between Sir Roger de Coverley, the mouthpiece of the old landed gentry, and Sir Andrew Freeport, the typical city merchant, had set forth the claims of commerce in an even more specific form. Defoe in *Roxana* had eulogized the "true-bred Merchant" as "the best gentleman in the Nation," and Steele in *The Conscious Lovers* had struck the same note on the stage: "Sir," says his Mr. Sealand, "as much a Cit as you take me for, I know the town and the world; and give me leave to say that we merchants are a species of gentry, that have grown into the world this last century, and are as honourable, and almost as useful, as you landed folks, that have always thought yourselves so much above us." The prosings of Thorowgood, stilted and dull as they are, have therefore, as we can now see, a specific significance which reinforces the general significance of the play as a whole.

Then, secondly, the moral purpose of *The London Merchant* has been emphasized. Lillo's didacticism was no accidental characteristic of his work; it was, as his own declaration has shown us, primary and fundamental; the ethical utility of tragedy being for him the starting point and justification of his new experiment in the drama. Now the gradual moralization of English literature during the eighteenth century was in the main the result of the spreading influence of the middle classes and their Puritan spirit. We perceive the direct effect of this in Lillo, as we perceive it in Richardson. To put *The London Merchant* into its proper place, we have to remember that in it, practically for the first time on the English boards since the fat days of the Restoration, youthful weakness and profligacy are presented not as a theme for merrymaking and loose laughter, but as illustrations of the truth that whoso sows the wind shall reap the whirlwind for his harvest.

Finally, we must take note of the peculiar

tone and quality of Lillo's moral teaching. It is not only Puritan; it is also in the last degree utilitarian. We have seen that for years *The London Merchant* was much patronized by the "Mercantile Interest," whose influence was largely responsible for its annual revival at Christmas time. We need not wonder at this. Lillo's drama is something more than a homily on the dangers of licentiousness. It is a sermon on dishonesty and on the virtues which are essential for success in a commercial career -- virtues of which aristocratic literature had never deigned to take cognizance. A typical evangelical writer of the early nineteenth century—Vicessimus Knox—in his advice to "those destined for a mercantile life," warns his readers against novels and plays, because "they almost invariably represent the virtues of a trader, such as honesty, sobriety, punctuality, and industry, as contemptible and ridiculous"; but he makes an exception in favor of *The London Merchant.* The reason is clear. In *The London Merchant* these very qualities are kept to the front. Hogarth, whose own work was itself a product of the same changing social conditions, some years later showed the ingenuous youth of his day the contrasted ways of virtue and vice; the one leading to wealth, honor, and high place; the other to poverty, misery, and the jail. Lillo had already enforced the same sublime truth in his own artless fashion. Honesty is the best policy for all concerned; be honest and you will not be hanged, but may even live to become "a very eminent merchant." We can well imagine the natural anxiety of the "Mercantile Interest" that all youths and apprentices should "mind the moral," when such gems of wisdom as these were clearly enunciated by the actors with an eye to the twopenny gallery:

"Business requires our attendance; business, the youth's best preservative from ill, as idleness his worst of snares";

and

"Method in business is the surest guide. He who neglects it frequently stumbles, and always wanders perplexed, uncertain, and in danger."

Such were the precepts which the embryo merchant was desired to lay to heart. "Since," wrote the German translator of Lillo's play, "in every great commercial city there are so many Barnwells who are walking thoughtlessly in a similar path of destruction, may his picture be to all young men who devote themselves to commerce, an example of horror and detestation! And may they, on the other hand, take the honest Trueman, that trustworthy and industrious clerk, for their imitation."

Take heed, young men of the twopenny gallery, and when you are tempted to pilfer, to neglect your business, or to go philandering, remember the fate of George Barnwell!

VIII

In view of the immense success of *The London Merchant* it seems strange that Lillo's direct influence on the English drama should have been so small. The stage is always on the lookout for fresh sensations, and one might well have supposed that there would be playwrights in plenty to follow his lead; the more so, that the vein of conventional tragedy was by this time clearly exhausted. As a matter of fact, however, the plays produced in England during the eighteenth century which stand in the actual line of his work may be counted on the fingers of one hand. Of these, two only have any importance—Edward Moore's *The Gamester,* which together with *The London Merchant* carried the new style of English drama to the Continent, and, much better as a play than either though of far less historical interest, *The Mysterious Husband* of

Richard Cumberland. The further evolution of Domestic Tragedy must be followed, not in England, but in France and Germany, and in the works of such writers as La Chaussèe, Landois, Diderot, Sedaine, Mercier, Beaumarchais, and Lessing. In England its history ultimately became involved with that of the influence of German melodrama at the close of the eighteenth century.

How are we to account for the failure of Domestic Tragedy to establish itself as a recognized type on the English stage? Several reasons may be suggested. I will here confine myself to two.

To begin with, there is the fact that no writer of marked genius and power — no one of the caliber of Diderot or Lessing — took up the new form. We have seen that the popularity of *The London Merchant* at the time of its production and for some years afterward is to be explained without the slightest reference to the inherent merits of the play, which was too crude and poor either to survive among the fittest things in the struggle for existence when its temporary vogue was over, or even to furnish a satisfactory model for later dramatists; while *The Gamester,* though a more respectable performance, was similarly lacking in the qualities necessary for permanent success. It

159

is perhaps desirable that the student of the
evolution of literature should occasionally
remind himself of the truism (which as an
evolutionist he may too easily forget) that
whatever importance he is inclined to attach
to environment and general conditions, no
great work of art, after all, is possible unless
we have the great artist. I do not doubt that
Lillo's lead might have been followed by the
creation of a new and living form of drama had
the right man arisen along with the opportunity. But the right man did not arise.
If Fielding, for example, whose sympathies,
as we have learned, were largely with it, had
devoted to Domestic Drama the powers which
afterwards went to the making of *Amelia*,
the history of that drama would, I believe,
have been different. It would, I venture to
think, have been different if Richardson had
written *Clarissa* (in which he himself saw the
materials of a fine tragedy) for the stage
instead of for the reading public. As it was,
the new type remained in the hands of men of
mediocre talents, and thus, while it indirectly
influenced the theory and practice of the
drama in various ways, in itself for the time
being it came to nothing.

If we now ask why, despite their avowed
interest in it, Fielding and Richardson were

not attracted to the Domestic Drama, the answer, of course, is that their energies were preoccupied by other work; and this introduces us to a second reason for the sterility of Lillo's experiment. At the time when the new drama arose, the creative powers which might otherwise have found their field on the stage were drawn off into the novel. Now the novel, as I have been solicitous to show, was itself the product of precisely the same influences in life and literature as had inspired *The London Merchant* and *The Gamester;* but apart altogether from the fact that the general tendencies of the time favored its growth at the expense of the drama, it offered in comparison a far better channel for the rising democratic spirit. Professor Minto has argued that the enormous and ever-growing popularity of prose fiction was a chief cause of the decline of poetry in England during the second half of the eighteenth century. This is highly probable. It is certain that it was a chief cause of the decline of the drama, and the general decline of the drama manifestly militated powerfully in its turn against the further development of the middle-class serious play. Thus, so far as England is concerned, the influence of the new spirit in literature, at the time when that spirit was fast growing in volume and range, has to be sought rather in prose fiction than on the stage.

What, then, of Lillo's permanent importance in the history of the European drama? That he was an interesting figure in the literature of his own time should now, I think, be apparent; but it may still be urged that he belonged to his own time only. Taking the largest view of the significance of his work, however, we may fairly contend that it was at least germinal. If his attempt to enlarge the scope of tragedy and to bring it into touch with the realities of actual life had little immediate result in England, the impulse which he gave to Continental writers shows that it was by no means abortive. It is by following the development of Domestic Tragedy through their writings that we can best understand that, isolated and ineffective as he seems at first sight to be, he was in fact a forerunner both of what to-day we loosely call melodrama and, more important than this, of that social play of realistic character and serious purpose which is so prominent a feature of our modern stage.

SAMUEL RICHARDSON: THE FATHER
OF THE ENGLISH NOVEL

I

I HAVE insisted in the foregoing essay that
from the point of view of the social significance of literature there is a close connection
between Lillo's abortive experiment in the
Domestic Drama and the beginnings of that
new kind of prose fiction which we specifically
call the modern novel: both, as I have shown,
being indications of the fast-rising influence of
the middle classes in the early decades of the
eighteenth century. It is natural, therefore, to
turn from the author of *The London Merchant*
to the author of *Pamela*—from the playwright
who set London weeping over the downfall
of "an odious apprentice boy" to the novelist
who wrought all England up to wild enthusiasm with his story of the trials and triumph
of a lady's maid. Of course the contrast between these two men is very striking. Lillo
was one of the obscurest of eighteenth-century
writers; he is treated by historians with neglect
or contempt; it is difficult to-day to obtain for
him even the moderate recognition which is
really his due. Richardson, on the other hand,
was one of the most prominent figures in his

age; he occupies many pages in the annals of literature, and the actual value of his work has been exaggerated rather than under-rated. Yet despite the prestige of his name and the continual repetition of the commonplaces of criticism regarding him, it is after all doubtful whether outside the narrow circle of professed students of literature he is much better known —known, I mean, at first hand—than Lillo. We often hear people reproducing what other people have said about the tragic power of *Clarissa;* but we may well wonder how many of these glib retailers of borrowed opinions have ever gone steadily through that voluminous work, I will not say four times, like the author's admiring correspondent, Margaret Collier, but just once. Richardson made his appeal to a more leisured generation than ours, and it is not surprising that we now recoil from the appalling prolixity of his writings. Who was the too-outspoken critic who once defined a classic as a book which we talk about but do not read? To be equally candid, I fear that Richardson's novels have long since become classics in this melancholy sense. They keep their place of dignity on our shelves; we look at them with respect and wax eloquent over their merits; but we leave them undisturbed and seek our amusement elsewhere.

It is not, however, to be denied that they retain a sort of shadowy power over our imaginations; we do continue to talk about them; and this is more than can be said for the plays of Lillo, which are thus everlastingly excluded even from the cynic's category of the classical. And this fact provides the motive of the present essay. Obviously, there is not the same reason for writing about Richardson as there is for writing about Lillo. But there is another reason for doing so, and one which is perhaps quite as good. For if the oblivion into which the dramatist has fallen may be held to justify the modest effort which I have made to reinstate him among the writers of his time, the interest which still clings about the name of the novelist may just as fittingly serve as an excuse for a brief and informal study of the man and his work.

II

Samuel Richardson was born in 1689, and was thus a year younger than Pope. Like Lillo he came of the "middling" class, his father being a joiner and, as he tells us, a "very honest man," his mother "a good woman, of family not ungenteel." He received a common-school education only, learning no language but his own, and, as his style subsequently

showed, having no very rigorous training
even in that. A shy and sensitive boy,
caring nothing for play, and grave in manner
beyond his years, he was naturally an object
of derision to his school fellows. But he had
his own way of winning their affection. He
told them stories, partly from memory of
what he had read or heard, partly of his own
invention. All these stories, he afterwards
declared, "carried with them, I am bold to
say, a useful moral." Already the didactic
turn of his mind was pronounced; and though
he makes no reference to the fact, we may
safely surmise that long-windedness was another
characteristic of these early essays in fiction.

The elder Richardson was at first ambitious
that his son should enter the church, and it was
only want of money that compelled him to
relinquish this design. But if his hortatory
talents were thus lost to the ministry, they
were not, as the sequel showed, to be lost to
the world at large. "Charles," said Coleridge
on one occasion, to his friend Lamb, "you
never heard me preach, did you?" "My dear
C-C-Coleridge," stammered Lamb in reply,
"I have n-n-never heard you do anything
else." The application of this anecdote to
Richardson's case is obvious.

All thought of the church abandoned, Samuel

166

at seventeen was apprenticed to a printer and stationer named Wilde, a hard man, though of good standing in his business. As an apprentice the future novelist soon showed his mettle. He might indeed have stood as the painter's model for the good young man in Hogarth's famous series of sermon-plates; for according to his own account of himself, his industry, his honesty, his desire for self-improvement, and at the same time his punctilious attention to his master's interests left nothing to be desired. "I stole from the hours of rest and relaxation my reading times for improvement of my mind," he tells us; and yet, as he is solicitous to add, "I took care that even my candle was of my own purchasing, that I might not, in the most trifling instance, make my master a sufferer." His scruples went even further than this; he made it a rule never to sit up so late over his studies as to impair his strength for the proper performance of his duties on the following day.

His apprenticeship over, he became first a compositor and then a proofreader, and in 1719 set up in business for himself in Fleet Street, moving thence a little later to Salisbury Court (now Salisbury Square), where he continued to have his town quarters to the end of his life. In the orthodox fashion of the good apprentice, he took as his first wife his master's daughter, and when he married again he still kept loyally to the trade by choosing the daughter of a bookseller in Bath. He throve greatly in business, climbing the commercial ladder rung by rung, gaining the respect of all with whom he had dealings in the city, and in due course becoming one of the king's printers and Master of Stationers Hall. These details have their value for the light which they throw upon the character of the man and, through that, upon his writings. His attitude toward trade is also instructive. He was not in the least ashamed of printer's ink or of the snug little fortune which it enabled him to accumulate. Yet he still recognized that business is one thing and what his century called the *beau monde* quite another. He accepted without demur the caste divisions of his time. For him it was part of the divinely appointed order that Temple Bar should represent a social as well as a geographical line of demarkation between two sharply divided worlds; east of it lay the city; west, the sacred regions of fashionable life. And it is worth while to remember that as a novelist he was always something of a "cit," and was never really at home west of Temple Bar. This was fully understood by good judges at

the time. Lady Mary Wortley Montague
declared that she cried like a milkmaid (why
milkmaid?) over *Clarissa,* but that Richardson had "no idea of the manners of high
life." Chesterfield said that he "mistook the
modes." Walpole made a similar criticism.
Such strictures from such authorities must be
regarded as final. Richardson in fact was limited in experience and outlook by the bound-
aries of the class to which he belonged.

He continued to live entirely at his business
premises in Salisbury Court for many years,
and then, growing prosperity warranting the
course, he took a house in what was then the
country, in order to have a quiet resting place
to which to retire for what we should now call
his "week ends." His first choice was a substantial residence in North End Road, Fulham,
"a few paces," as he tells a correspondent,
"from Hammersmith Turnpike." There he
lived till 1754, when he moved a little farther
out to Parson's Green, Fulham. By this
time, it must be remembered, he was something
more than a successful printer and "warm"
man of affairs. He was a celebrated author—a
novelist whose reputation was already European. At Parson's Green, his work done and
the responsibilities of Salisbury Court largely
left behind him, he was free to enjoy both his

leisure and his fame. We picture him there, the center of a little circle of fervent admirers (mostly feminine) luxuriating in the flattery which was freely poured upon him, and spending his closing years, in purring contentment, in what Mr. Gosse has called a kind of perpetual tea party. "The great author," says Thackeray, "was accustomed to be adored. A gentler wind never puffed mortal vanity. Enraptured spinsters flung tea leaves round him, and incensed him with the coffee pot. Matrons kissed the slippers they had worked for him. There was a halo of virtue round his nightcap. All Europe had thrilled, panted, admired, trembled, wept, over the pages of the immortal little kind honest man with the round paunch."

Unfortunately, dark shadows gathered about him in the decline of his life. He had always suffered from indifferent health and wretched nerves, and though he had taken the utmost care of himself—for a long time he was a teetotaler and a vegetarian—his sedentary habits and aversion to fresh air and exercise ultimately told upon him, and the hypochondria and extreme irritability which made him miserable toward the last are thus easily explained. He died of a stroke of apoplexy in 1761.

Richardson had all the qualities of an excellent man of business, for he was industrious, painstaking, and shrewd, absolutely straightforward in all his dealings, and honest to the finger tips. No man in the city of London was more keenly alive than he to the value of a penny, or practiced more persistently the homely virtues of thrift and prudence. Yet he was kind to his workpeople — according to tradition, it was a little trick of his to hide a half-crown piece among the types in the composing room so that the first man to arrive might find it and thus gain a reward for his diligence — and he was generous to struggling authors (he once, at least, came to the rescue of Johnson during the latter's days of poverty), and this is a trait which in a successful printer and writer may be held to cover a multitude of sins. Though his home life was marked by a good deal of formality and austerity, he was an affectionate husband and father and he had a happy faculty of winning the love and confidence of children. Perhaps his least admirable characteristic was his inordinate vanity, which grew with his fame and was stimulated by the adulation of his little coterie of female worshipers. An incident recorded by Boswell is to the point here. One day in a large company which was assembled for dinner in the house in North End, "a gentleman who had just returned from Paris, wishing to please Mr. Richardson, mentioned to him a very flattering circumstance—that he had seen his *Clarissa* lying on the king's brother's table. Richardson, observing that part of the company were engaged in talking to each other, affected then not to attend to it. But by and by, when there was a general silence and he thought that the flattery might be fully heard, he addressed himself to the gentleman: 'I think, sir, you were saying something about—' pausing in a high flutter of expectation." But the gentleman, perceiving that his host was fishing for compliments, mischievously resolved to disappoint him. "A mere trifle, sir," he replied, with an exquisitely sly air of indifference. Richardson's mortification, Boswell adds, "was visible, and he did not speak ten words more the whole day." We can well understand Boswell's further statement that Johnson, who was present, hugely enjoyed the joke. Entirely self-centered and self-involved, Richardson had, as Johnson by this time had discovered, only one topic of conversation—his own books; and in regard to these he could tolerate only unqualified praise; the slightest hint of adverse criticism upset him completely. His childish jealousy of other successful authors, and notably of his most dangerous rival, Fielding, was of course only one phase of his consuming vanity. Perhaps we cannot wonder that he never forgave the writer of *Joseph Andrews* for his mercilessly severe and irreverent handling of *Pamela*. But even his natural irritation, while it may explain, certainly does not excuse, the petty spitefulness which he exhibited in all his remarks upon his great contemporary. He thought Fielding hopelessly vulgar; called his work "wretchedly low and dirty"; declared that "his brawls, his jars, his jails, his sponging-houses, were all drawn from what he had seen and known"; and worst of all, roundly abused *Amelia* while obstinately refusing to read it. The two men—the one so finicky and sensitive, the other so full-blooded and robustious—were indeed so diametrically opposed in temper and character that no common ground of understanding and sympathy could ever have been found between them. It is not our business here to adjust their differences. But it is well to realize that Fielding possessed in abundance the quality which Richardson most conspicuously lacked —virility. Hazlitt once described Rogers as a very lady-like poet. Without sarcasm, we may call Richardson a very lady-like man.

III

Till he reached fifty, our fat, honest, pragmatical little printer had pursued his quiet and prosperous way of life without dreaming of the greatness that was in store for him. He had from time to time at their request provided his friends among the publishers with prefaces and dedications for their works; but such things of course gave no indication of his genius either to himself or to others; and thus far he was aware of no promptings toward the more ambitious kinds of authorship. Had he died at fifty, therefore, you and I would have known nothing about him, and a great page in the history of eighteenth-century literature would have remained unwritten. Then by one of the most curious flukes recorded in the annals of letters, he accidentally "slipped," according to his own expression, into the production of an epoch-making book.

To understand how this came about we must consider in some detail the lines along which he unconsciously advanced toward the work which was to bring him immediate and lasting fame.

I have already referred to his boyish propensity for story-telling. This, manifestly, is itself an important fact. But to this must now be added his precocious proficiency in the

174

feminine accomplishment of letter writing — a perfect mania for which continued all through his life. "From my earliest youth," he tells us, "I had a love of letter writing"; and he goes on to relate that this love on one occasion led to an incident which he rightly regarded as prophetic.

"I was not eleven years old when I wrote spontaneously, a letter to a widow of near fifty, who, pretending to a zeal for religion, and being a constant frequenter of church-ordinances, was continually fomenting quarrels and disturbances, by back-biting and scandal, among all her acquaintai ce. I collected from the Scripture, exts that mai'e against her. Assuming the style a d address of a person in years, I exhorted her, I ei ostulated with her. But my hand-writing was known. I was challenged with it, and owned the boldness; for she complained of it to my mother with tears. My mother chid me for the freedom taken by such a boy with a woman of her years; but knowing that her son was not of a pert or forward nature, but on the contrary shy and bashful, she commended my principles, though she censured the liberty taken."

Pretty good, this, for a boy "not eleven years old"! In this little bit of autobiography, written, as will be seen, with characteristic self-complacency, Richardson the child stands revealed to us as father of Richardson the man.

But his letter-writing faculty had results

far more important than this. It brought him into close relations with women, and so helped him to acquire that extraordinary knowledge of the mysterious thing which sentimental novelists call "the female heart," which is one of the outstanding features of his work. This, too, is a point upon which he afterwards laid stress.

"As a bashful, and not forward boy, I was an early favourite with all the young women of taste and reading in the neighbourhood. Half-a-dozen of them, when met to work with their needles, used, when they got a book they liked, and thought I should, to borrow me to read to them, and both mothers and daughters used to be pleased with the observations they put me upon making. . . . I was not more than thirteen when three of these young women, unknown to each other, having an high opinion of my taciturnity, revealed to me their love-secrets, in order to induce me to give them copies to write after, or correct, for answers to their lovers' letters, nor did any of them ever know that I was secretary of the others. I have been directed to chide and even repulse, when an offence was either taken or given, at the very time that the heart of the chider or repulser was open before me, overflowing with esteem and affection, and the fair repulser, dreading to be taken at her word, directing *this* word or *that* expression to be softened or changed. One, highly gratified with her lover's fervour and vows of everlasting love, has said, when I asked her direction, 'I cannot tell you what to write, but (her heart on her lips) you cannot write too kindly'; all her fear was only that she should incur slight for her kindness."

That as a boy of thirteen—an age when the ordinary human male is particularly impervious to the attractions of the other sex—Richardson should have been chosen and should have been willing to act as the confidant and adviser of three young women in love, and should have performed his delicate functions to their entire satisfaction, is a fact of capital importance as illustrating both his precocity and the peculiar bias of his mind. But it is even more significant as showing the curious way in which, while still very young, he was being prepared for his future work. He received his early training, not through books or literary discipline, but by direct contact with certain phases of life; he thus gained knowledge which no amount of mere scholarship would ever have given him; and what is more, his insight was quickened and his sympathies engaged, while in placing his pen at the service of his fair friends and exercising it in their behalf, he learned how to impart to his letter writing something of a dramatic character, and to make it the vehicle of ideas and sentiments other than his own.

The qualities and powers which such experiences helped to develop long lay latent and unsuspected, as we have seen. But the time came when they were to be turned to account.

In 1739, as he himself records, two book-sellers of London — "my particular friends" (their names, by the way, were Rivington and Osborne) — entreated him "to write for them a little volume of letters, in the common style, on such subjects as might be of use to those country readers, who were unable to indite for themselves." The two publishers were doubtless well aware of Richardson's passion for letter writing, and were thus led to proffer their request. At any rate the commission was entirely in his line, and he accepted it with avidity. But if his passion for letter writing was strong, so also was his passion for edification; and it occurred to him that he might turn the humble venture he had taken in hand to the moral as well as to the intellectual advantage of his readers. "Will it be any harm," he said to his friends, "in a piece you want to be written so low, if we should teach them how they should think and act in common cases, as well as indite?" Rivington and Osborne "were the more urgent with me to begin the little volume from this hint." So he set about his task and soon wrote "two or three letters to instruct handsome girls, who were obliged to go out to service, as we phrase it, how to avoid the snares that might be laid against their virtue."

While he was engaged on these, it chanced that a true story, which had been told him many years before by a friend, came into his mind; and, he continues, in the letter to Aaron Hill from which the foregoing quotations have been made:

"I thought the story, if written in an easy and natural manner, suitably to the simplicity of it, might possibly introduce a new species of writing, that might possibly turn young people into a course of reading different from the pomp and parade of romance writing, and dismissing the improbable and marvellous with which novels generally abound, might tend to promote the cause of religion and virtue. I therefore gave way to enlargement, and so *Pamela* became what you see her."

Such was the origin of the first of our modern novels, in the sense in which the word novel is now understood; that is, the first sustained work of fiction in which the machinery of the older romances, heroic and picaresque, is discarded, and the interest is made to center, not in the adventures of princes, shepherds, vagabonds, or criminals, but in the lives and experiences of men and women belonging to the ordinary contemporary social world. That such a book should have been the result of a happy accident — a kind of by-product of a Complete Letter Writer — is of course the one fact in its history which is most certain to

arrest attention. Yet we must be careful not
to make too much of the fortuitous character
of the undertaking. As Richardson's own
statement shows, he was fully conscious of
experimenting in a "new species" of composition. From the outset, therefore, he realized
the importance of his innovation. [1]

IV

It is not, I think, generally known that the
volume of Familiar Letters out of which *Pamela*
sprang was itself presently finished and published. Few readers of Richardson, in all
probability, have ever troubled themselves
to dip into its pages, for a Letter Writer is
not commonly regarded as a very attractive
kind of literature. But it has some interest
in connection with our author's peculiar
methods and principles.

In accordance with its twofold aim, this
volume contains, on the one hand, "forms to
be observed in writing familiar letters," and
on the other, instructions "how to think and
act justly and prudently in the common concerns of human life." Its most remarkable

[1] In regard to *Pamela* there has been the inevitable discussion as
to "sources." It has been suggested that Richardson may have
owed something to Marivaux's *Marianne*, an English translation of
which was published in 1736. The story of Amanda and the
wicked young lord of the manor in the 375th *Spectator* is also
supposed to have given him hints. But even if such indebtednesses
could be proved, he is still entitled to the honor which belongs to
the independent discoverer.

feature, however, is the quite surprising range
of its subject matter. We find in it, as we
might expect, applications to parents for their
daughter's hand, declarations of diffident
wooers, letters of condolence which "with
small variations may be used to a husband on
the death of his wife, and on other melancholy
occasions of the like nature." But along with
these we have also warnings to young women
on the dangers of London; advice to apprentices to obey their masters; demands of creditors for the payment of debts; petitions of
distressed debtors for merciful treatment.
Even in preparing his Letter Writer, therefore,
Richardson was still the moralist and the man
of business. Two features of the collection
are, however, specially important. One is,
that a very large place is given in it to questions
of love, courtship, and marriage; the other,
that the letters often expand beyond their
nominal purpose into essays-in-little in the
art of description, narrative, and characterization. There is one, for example, from a
villager to a friend abroad, which conveys the
news that "John Jones, the organist, is married
to Sykes' daughter, Peggy, who proves an
arrant shrew, and has broke about his head his
best Cremona fiddle, in the sight of half-a-
dozen neighbours." Such a letter can hardly

be meant as a "form" to be followed, for the
circumstances imagined are, it is to be hoped,
too exceptional; nor is its value as an exhibition
of the evils of ill-assorted marriages or of
shrewishness particularly evident. It is in
fact a bit of comedy which might just as well
have found its place in the pages of *Pamela*.
Many of these letters indeed need only proper
setting to become scenes in a regular story.
I will give one—a very amusing one—in illustration. It is written by a "disdainful
damsel" with reference to her not very welcome suitor.

"The first time the honest man came to see me, in
the way you were pleased to put into his head, was on
Sunday after sermon time. He began by telling me;
what I found at my finger ends, that it was very cold;
and politely blowed on his. I immediately perceived
that his passion for me could not keep him warm;
and in complaisance to your recommendation, con-
ducted him to the fireside. After he had pretty
well rubbed heat into his hands, he stood up with his
back to the fire, and with his hand behind him, held
up his coat, that he might be warm all over; and,
looking about him, asked with the tranquillity of a
man a twelvemonth married, and just come off a
journey, 'How all friends did in the country?' I said;
I hoped very well, but would be glad to warm my
fingers.' 'Cry mercy, madam,' and then he shuffled
a little further from the fire, and after two or three
hems and a long pause, 'I have heard,' said he, 'a
most excellent sermon just now. Dr. Thomas is a fine

man truly. Did you ever hear him, madam?' 'No, sir, I generally go to my own parish church.' 'That's right, madam, to be sure. What was your subject to-day?' 'The Pharisee and the Publican, sir.' 'A very good one truly. Dr. Thomas would have made a fine work on that subject. His text to-day was— *Evil communications corrupt good manners.*' 'A good subject, sir. I doubt not that the doctor made a fine discourse upon it.' 'O, ay, madam, he can't make a bad one on any subject.' I ran for the tea-kettle, for, thought I, we shall have all the heads of the sermon immediately. At last came the happy moment of his taking leave, for I would not ask him to stay supper. And then, though I had an opportunity of saying little more than *yes* and *no* at the time, for he took the vapours he had put me into for devotion or gravity (at least, I believe), he pressed my hand, looked frightfully kind, and gave me to understand that if, upon further conversation and inquiry into my character, he should happen to like me as well as he did from my behaviour and person, why truly I need not fear in time being blessed with him for my husband."

As an episode from the comedy of courtship this is capital. But it is by no means clear what purpose such an effusion is supposed to serve in a volume designed for the use of " those country readers who were unable to indite for themselves." Was it the author's aim to sharpen their wits as well as to improve their characters and their style? Did he intend his "disdainful damsel" to provide encouragement

to young ladies in like case to take care
of themselves and poke fun at their awkward
lovers? We need not doubt that he was true
to his didactic principles in framing this epistle.
But it is evident, I think, that he was carried
away by the possibilities of the situation he
had devised, and the letter in consequence has
all the qualities which characterize the work
of Richardson the novelist. It might well indeed have come from the lively pen of Miss
Anna Howe.

V

To return to *Pamela*. Once embarked upon
his undertaking, Richardson's progress was
rapid. While engaged upon it, he tells us, he
read it portion by portion to his "worthy-
hearted wife" and a young lady friend who
was then staying with them, who used to drop
into his "little closet" every evening with the
question — "Have you any more of Pamela,
Mr. R.? We are come to hear a little more
of Pamela." Thus encouraged, he made such
headway with his task that the original two
volumes, begun, according to his memorandum,
on November 10, 1739, were finished on January 10 following: not a bad record for an
author who was meanwhile immersed in "other
business."

Published early in 1740, the work scored an
instant and enormous success—a success which
must indeed have exceeded Richardson's wild-
est expectations, for he had written it for
"young people" in his own "middling" class,
and behold! it also conquered the critics and
brought the aristocratic world to his feet.
Pope—the great Pope himself—praised it; the
chaplain of St. Saviour's, Southwark, recommended it from the pulpit—undoubtedly the
first time that any piece of fiction had been so
distinguished; fashionable ladies, it is said,
carried it with them to their routs and mas-
querades; not to have read *Pamela*, the
Gentleman's Magazine declared, was judged
by "the Town" as "great a sign of want of
curiosity" as "not to have seen the French and
Italian dancers." One evidence of this popularity was the appearance before the year was
out of a spurious continuation entitled *Pamela
in High Life.* This in itself has no value; but
it is indirectly important because it prompted
Richardson's own sequel, now unfortunately
to be considered an essential part of his work.
In regard to this sequel, Pope and his satellite
Warburton had advised him "to make it a
vehicle for satire upon the follies and fashions
of the great world, by representing the light
in which they would appear to the rustic

Pamela when she was introduced to them."
Had Richardson possessed the required knowledge of "the great world," the suggestion
would have been excellent; but he did not, and
realizing his deficiencies, he wisely left the
matter alone.   But he made as great a mistake
in another way.   He allowed his didactic tendency to have its full fling, and the second part
of *Pamela* is in effect a ponderous and wearisome treatise on domestic relationships, the
upbringing of children, and kindred themes.

Let us glance at the book which suddenly
transformed the little printer into one of the
most famous authors of his day.   We call it
simply *Pamela*, but it is well to remember its
original full title, which is not only a program
but also an advertisement and a declaration
of faith: *Pamela; or Virtue Rewarded. In a
Series of Familiar Letters from a Beautiful Young
Damsel to her Parents. Published in order to
Cultivate the Principles of Virtue and Religion in
the Mind of the Youth of Both Sexes. A narrative
which has its Foundations in Truth; and at the
Same Time that it agreeably entertains by a Variety
of Curious and Affecting Incidents, is entirely
divested of all those Images which, in too many
Pieces calculated for Amusement only, tend to
inflame the Minds they should instruct.*   Reduced
to its bare outlines, the story introduced

by this prodigious preamble is as follows: Pamela Andrews is the handsome daughter of humble but God-fearing parents, who have trained her in the strictest ways of religion and virtue. She becomes lady's maid to a certain Mrs. B., who has a son, a good-looking and attractive young fellow, but unfortunately of "free principles." The inevitable happens; Mr. B. becomes enamored of his mother's pretty servant; and when Mrs. B. dies (her death forms the actual starting point of the narrative) he begins to pester her with his attentions, not, as may be imagined, for what the French call *le bon motif*. Pamela resists; but her resistance only adds fuel to his flame. Then under pretense of taking her on a visit to her parents, he beguiles her to a lonely house on his Lincolnshire estate, where his housekeeper, the vile Mrs. Jewkes, does all in her power to second his efforts. In this part of the story there is a great deal to remind us of the extraordinary difference in taste between Richardson's time and ours. He announced in his preface, and he did so of course with absolute sincerity, that his purpose was to make vice odious and virtue lovely "without raising a single idea throughout the whole book that shall shock the exactest purity." Yet the language used and the views expressed by Mrs. Jewkes in her many conversations with Pamela — conversations which the girl herself reproduces faithfully and in detail — are such as to take one's breath away when we encounter them in a book intended *virginibus puerisque.* Perhaps it will help us to get at the right point of view in regard to this matter if we remember that, while we are now disgusted by Smollett's grossness, Dean Delaney read *Roderick Random* aloud to his wife and *Peregrine Pickle* was one of the books borrowed by Lydia Languish from the circulating library. Another and more personal aspect of Richardson's work, suggested at this point, may also be touched on. All his characters have a craze for reducing everything to writing; they have all his own business-like habits and love of order and system. Thus Pamela in her imprisonment keeps an elaborate journal in which she records every incident and interview and in which she analyzes minutely her thoughts and feelings. Thus, too, Mr. B., not satisfied with verbal assaults, sends her a formal statement of his proposals, divided into "articles," which are numbered I to VII; while Pamela replies to him in a similar document, taking up his "articles" in sequence, one by one. For example, under VI, Mr. B. defines his position:

"Now, Pamela, will you see what a value I set upon the free-will of a person *already* in my power; and who, if these proposals are not accepted, shall find that I have not taken all these pains, and risked my reputation, as I have done, without resolving to gratify my passion for you at all adventures. And it will behoove you to consider whether it is not better for you to comply upon terms so advantageous to you, and so beneficial to your father and mother and other friends, than to be mine without condition or equivalent."

In answer to which Pamela defines *her* position, thus:

"I know, sir, by woful experience, that I am in your power; I know all the resistance I can make will be poor and weak, and perhaps stand me in little stead; I dread your *will* to ruin me is as great as your *power;* yet, sir, will I dare to tell you that I can make no free-will offering of my virtue. All I *can* do, poor as that may be, I will do, to preserve my honour; and then, if I cannot escape the violence of man, I can safely appeal to the great God my only refuge, with this consolation, that my will bore no part in my violation."

Nothing could be more regular and official than such an exchange of views; and in the circumstances, nothing surely could be more amazing.

Meanwhile, the story creeps slowly on from point to point. Pamela attempts to escape, but is deterred by a mad bull, by her fear of robbers, and so on. In her despair, she is almost driven to suicide. But at length her constancy and her sorrows touch her master's heart. He is moved to the pity which is akin to love. A true affection springs up in place of the false. He obtains by fair means what he could not gain by foul; and in the end, Pamela becomes the "happy, thrice happy" Mrs. B.

There are still persons, I believe, who profess to enjoy *Pamela.* For my own part I find it dreary stuff, though I admit that as a picture of manners—or more correctly, of certain phases of life seen from a certain point of view — it is not without interest. But if poor as a story, it is far worse as a tract. Its famous moral teaching, trumpeted abroad by the self-complacent author himself, and received with a general chorus of praise, will not in fact bear a moment's examination.

The fault does not lie with the theme of the book, or with its occasional coarseness and pruriency. These things, as I have said, belonged to Richardson's age, and may therefore be dismissed. It lies with the character of the heroine herself and her relations with her master. One does not want to be too hard upon her; but she is not the sort of young woman to provide a satisfactory text for the author's sermon. She is too self-conscious and calculating; too politic in her behavior toward her humble suitor, Mr. Williams, on the one hand, and her aristocratic persecutor on the other. Her shrewdness and prudence are in fact quite as much in evidence as her virtue; she acts correctly, it is true, but at the same time she plays her cards remarkably well. It is not apparent that she had any affection for Mr. B. to start with, and the eagerness with which she ultimately accepts him, and the fulsome expressions of gratitude in which she indulges, make a very unpleasant impression upon us at the close. Putting the matter on the lowest ground, we may question with Scott whether her example "is not as well calculated to encourage a spirit of rash enterprise as of virtuous resistance." From a higher standpoint we may justly complain of the cool and narrow utilitarianism which it would seem to be the author's main purpose to inculcate. Virtue rewarded! "Is the reward of virtue bread?" asked Pope. In Pamela's case it is an establishment and a coach-and-six.

Nor must the treatment of Mr. B.'s character be overlooked. *Pamela* was designed for the edification of the "youth of both sexes." What sort of inspiration and guidance would Richardson's young men readers be likely to find in this study of an utter profligate who, having exhausted all his arts in the vain pursuit of a helpless girl, discovers that he can get his way by the aid of a clergyman and the Bible, and becomes in the sequel "one of the best and most exemplary of men?" Richardson's whole conception of Mr. B. is vitiated through and through by the tradesman's spirit of sycophancy in respect of the upper classes. We are made to feel that there is one standard of conduct for the "quality" and another for ordinary folk. As Traill put it, Mr. B. has already a couple of good "places" on earth, and that he should desire a third in heaven is really highly creditable to him as a member of the aristocracy and a landowner. As Scott pointed out, he "does not seem to have incurred any severe censure among his neighbours for the villainies which he practised upon Pamela; she herself supposes them more than atoned for by his condescension in wedding her; and consents to receive into favour even the unwomanly and infamous Mrs. Jewkes because the old procuress had acted a part she should have been hanged for, at the command, forsooth, of a generous master!" In the same way old Gaffer Andrews expresses no indignation at the conduct of Mr. B. toward his daughter; he is simply overwhelmed by the honor which the reformed rake does to the family by making the girl his wife.[1]

Sir James Mackintosh tried hard to turn the edge of such adverse criticism by emphasizing the limitations of the author's plan. Richardson's purpose, he insisted, was simply "to dispose young women of low rank to good conduct by *such motives as will work*. The hope of marrying a squire, though profligate, is a powerful instrument. This is a low and homely morality, to be sure; but Richardson in this place aimed no higher." This is, I think, the best that can be said for the ethics of the book; but it would hardly justify us to-day in recommending it from the pulpit.

I may add that even at the time the teachings and tendencies of *Pamela* were not accepted without protest. Among professed moralists, good old Isaac Watts showed his sound common sense by raising a dissentient voice. But a more effective criticism was passed upon the book in a travesty entitled

---

[1] In the churchyard of a little village in Dorsetshire I once came across the following epitaph. It reminded me so much of Richardson that I transcribed it, and for the same reason I reproduce it here: "In memory of William Forder, who died July 21st, 1817, aged 54 years. His honesty, fidelity, and strict attention to the interests of his master and mistress, Francis Fane, Esq. and Mrs. Fane, for more than 30 years, are here recorded in testimony of their approbation and as an example to all those whom Providence may place in a similar situation." I could not help wondering, as I read this illuminating epitaph, whether, like the Boston clergyman in the anecdote, Francis Fane, Esq., and Mrs. Fane might not have to complain of the "rather mixed society" of heaven.

An Apology for the Life of Mrs. Shamela Andrews, in which the mingled piety and cunning of Richardson's heroine are pitilessly exposed. In one place, for example, she hears her master approaching, and upon this —

"I ran up into my room, and washed and dressed myself as well as I could, and put on my prettiest round-eared cap, and then I practised all my airs before the glass, and then I sat down and read a chapter in *The Whole Duty of Man.*"

This is cruel enough, in all conscience; but it is not without justification. We do not know who wrote this skit. Richardson chose to think it was Fielding, and perhaps he was right: the passage quoted is quite in the great novelist's style. At any rate Fielding a little later turned the batteries of his ridicule upon *Pamela* in the opening chapters of *Joseph Andrews,* which, as everybody is aware, was in its inception a parody of Richardson's book.

VI

Richardson was in no hurry to follow up his first success. It was not till 1747–48 that he published in installments — seven volumes in all — his second novel, *Clarissa, or the History of a Young Lady.*

There has been a good deal of wild talk about

Clarissa. Admiring critics in dealing with it have thrown their superlatives about with a lavish hand. It has been placed in the front rank of English novels. Its heroine has been pronounced the most living woman in the whole range of fiction. Even its clumsy plot has been eulogized as "a model of ingenuity and artifice." Such praise seems to me reckless and absurd. Yet *Clarissa* is certainly a very remarkable work. It is not only Richardson's masterpiece, but also one of the outstanding novels of the eighteenth century.

Clarissa Harlowe is the beautiful daughter of an English country gentleman, and a young lady, according to Richardson's own description, "of great delicacy, mistress of all the accomplishments, natural and acquired, of the sex, having the strictest notion of filial duty." Her father is a domestic tyrant, who regards his authority over his family as unlimited, and whose temper is stern and unrelenting; her mother, a weak though well-meaning woman, who is distressed by her husband's severity, but has not strength of mind enough to make a stand against him. Clarissa, however, is not the only child of her parents. She has a surly brother named James, and a mean and disagreeable sister, Arabella, who dislikes her because of her superior beauty, and because she [Arabella] has been passed over in Clarissa's favor by their grandfather Harlowe in the distribution of his little property. This dislike is intensified into hatred when, just before the drama opens, Robert Lovelace, the chief male character of the piece, and, as we soon learn, a scoundrel of the deepest dye, transfers his suit from Arabella to Clarissa. A duel between James Harlowe and Lovelace, in which the former is wounded in the arm, had been one consequence of this action. Its more important result, however, is to be sought in Arabella's bitter jealousy of her sister.

One can conceive poor Clarissa's unhappiness under such conditions and in such surroundings. But the sum of her misery is not yet complete. Her brutal father is determined to force her into marriage with a wealthy suitor, a contemptible fellow named Solmes, and he stops at nothing in his effort to bend her will to his own. This is Lovelace's opportunity. He professes to come to her rescue. The day fixed for the hated marriage draws near. In desperation she throws herself upon his protection. Only when it is too late does she discover how thoroughly she has been deceived in him. He promises to convey her for safety to the house of a relative—a mere trick to get her into his power. He actually takes her to the establishment of a certain Mrs. Sinclair, who is simply Mrs. Jewkes over again, though in an even more infamous form. It is indicative of the poverty of Richardson's invention that he should thus have to fall back upon the machinery of his previous novel. The deceived and defenseless heroine — her profligate lover — his scheme to entrap her — the vile subordinates, his creatures, who help him to carry it out: all these, though much strengthened in the presentation, are obviously repeated from *Pamela*.

Clarissa is now Lovelace's prisoner, as Pamela had been Mr. B.'s; but the persecution which she has to undergo is a thousand times more diabolical than that to which her predecessor had been subjected. At length she contrives to escape, and takes lodgings with a Mrs. Moore, in Upper Flask Walk, Hampstead. But Lovelace' servant, Will Summers, tracks her out, and Lovelace himself, cleverly disguising himself as an old and gouty man (he is, among many other things, an accomplished actor), repairs to Mrs. Moore's house, ostensibly in search of apartments, and so surprises and recaptures his victim. He thus describes the incident to his friend and confidant, Belford:

"I saw it was impossible to conceal myself longer
from her, any more than (from the violent impulses
of my passion) to forbear manifesting myself. I un-
buttoned therefore my cape; I pulled off my flapped
slouched hat; I threw open my great-coat, and, like the
devil in Milton (an odd comparison, though!)

> I started up in my own form divine,
> Touched by the beam of her celestial eye,
> More potent than Ithuriel's spear.

"Now, Belford, for a similitude — now for a likeness
to illustrate the surprising scene, and the effect it had
upon my charmer and the gentlewoman! But nothing
was like it, or equal to it. The plain fact can only
describe it, or equal it. Thus then take it.

"She no sooner saw who it was than she gave three
violent screams, and before I could catch her in my
arms (as I was about to do the moment I discovered
myself) down she sunk at my feet in a fit; which made
me curse my indiscretion for so suddenly, and with so
much emotion, revealing myself.

"The gentlewoman, seeing so strange an alteration
in my person, and features, and voice, and dress, cried
out 'Murder, help! murder, help!' by turns, for half
a dozen times running. This alarmed the house, and
up ran two servant-maids, and my servant after them.
I cried out for water and hartshorn, and everyone flew
a different way, one of the maids as fast down as she
came up; while the gentlewoman ran out of one room
into another, and by turns up and down the apartment
we were in, without meaning or end, wringing her
foolish hands, and not knowing what she did.

"Up then came running a gentleman and his sister,
fetched and brought in by the maid, who had run down,
and having let in a cursed crabbed old wretch, hobbling

with his gout and mumbling with his hoarse, broken-toothed voice, who was metamorphosed all at once into a gay, lively young fellow, with a clear accent and all his teeth, she would have it that I was neither more nor less than the devil, and could not keep her eye from my foot, expecting no doubt every minute to see it discover itself to be cloven.

"For my part, I was so intent upon restoring my angel, that I regarded nobody else. And at last, she slowly recovering motion, with bitter sighs and sobs (only the whites of her eyes, however, appearing for some moments) I called upon her in the tenderest accents, as I kneeled by her, my arm supporting her head—'My angel! my charmer! my Clarissa! look upon me, my dearest life!—I am not angry with you.—I will forgive you, my best beloved!'

"The gentleman and his sister knew not what to make of all this; and the less when my fair one, recovering her sight, snatched another look at me, and then again groaned and fainted away."

Lovelace continues to describe the scene in the same minute fashion, but we must not now follow him further. Enough has been quoted to show that he has a wonderful eye for detail and is master of a graphic and vivacious style.

The climax of the tragedy is now reached. More determined and reckless than Mr. B., Lovelace does not scruple to resort to the vilest means to compass Clarissa's ruin. As Clarissa herself reports: "Under pretence of engaging me to make a visit in town," he "betrayed me back again to this vile house"—this is a fair description of Mrs. Sinclair's establishment—"where, again made a prisoner, I was first robbed of my senses and then of my honour."

But the villain himself does not go unscathed. Success does not bring him the satisfaction he had expected. Smitten with remorse (or something like it) he now offers his victim the one reparation in his power—marriage—only to find all his pleadings rejected with indignation. Finally Clarissa obtains her liberty. But her heart is broken, and she slowly pines away. After her death her persecutor reaps his reward; he is killed in a duel by her cousin, Colonel Morden.

Such is, in summary, the main plot of this oppressive and harrowing story, hundreds of pages of which are devoted to the evolution of Lovelace' tortuous schemes, to the tricks, deceptions, forgeries, and misrepresentations by which he ultimately attains his ends, and to the minute analysis of the long-drawn agony of the heroine' martyrdom. Repulsive it certainly is, and at times absolutely nauseating; but we cannot deny that in total effect it is extremely powerful. Happily the horror of the tragedy is to some extent relieved by the presence of a regular comedy sub-plot, the principal figure of which is Clarissa's friend, Anna Howe, a charming and vivacious girl, whose high spirits and irrepressible humor are like occasional bursts of sunshine amid the prevailing gloom.

Richardson's power depends so much on his peculiar method—the slow and laborious accumulation of details for the gradual creation of the impression he wishes to produce—that his art cannot quite fairly be represented by selections. But I will give one extract which will serve to illustrate his way of dealing with his materials. The scene I choose—that of Clarissa's death—is by the common consent of the critics one of the great scenes of the book. The reader may therefore feel assured that I am presenting our author at his best.

The narrative is contained in a letter from "Mr. Belford to Robert Lovelace, Esq.," dated simply "Thursday night." It is somewhat long; but length is of the essence of Richardson's art; and its typical quality would therefore be destroyed by curtailment.

"I may as well try to write; since, were I to go to bed, I shall not sleep. I never had such a weight of grief upon my mind in my life, as upon the demise of this admirable woman; whose soul is now rejoicing in the regions of light. You may be glad to know the particulars of her happy exit. I will try to proceed; for all is hush and still; the family retired; but not one of them, and least of all her poor cousin, I daresay, to rest. At four o'clock, as I mentioned in my last, I was sent for down; and as thou usedst to like my descriptions, I will give thee the woful scene that presented itself to me as I approached the bed. The Colonel was the first that took my attention, kneeling on the side of the bed, the lady's right hand in both his, which his face covered, bathing it with his tears; although she had been comforting him, as the woman since told me, in elevated strains, but broken accents.

"On the other side of the bed sat the good widow; her face overwhelmed with tears, leaning her head against the bed's head in a most disconsolate manner; and turning her face to me, as soon as she saw me—O Mr. Belford, cried she with folded hands—the dear lady—a heavy sob permitted her not to say more. Mrs. Smith, with clasped fingers and uplifted eyes, as if imploring help from the only power which could give it, was kneeling down at the bed's foot, tears in large drops trickling down her cheeks. Her nurse was kneeling between the widow and Mrs. Smith, her arms extended. In one hand she held an ineffectual cordial which she had just been offering her dying mistress; her face was swollen with weeping (though used to such scenes as this); and she turned her eyes towards me, as if she called upon me by them to join in the helpless sorrow, a fresh stream bursting from them as I approached the bed.

"The maid of the house with her face upon her folded arms, as she stood leaning against the wainscot, more audibly expressed her grief than any of the others. The lady had been silent a few minutes, and speechless; as they thought, moving her lips without uttering a word; one hand, as I said, in her cousin's. But when Mrs. Lovick, on my approach, pronounced my name—

O Mr. Belford, said she, with a faint inward voice, but very distinct nevertheless — Now — Now — (in broken periods she spoke). I bless God for his mercies to his poor creature — all will soon be over — a few — a very few moments — will end the strife — and I shall be happy. Comfort here, sir (turning her head to the Colonel) — comfort my cousin — see! the blameable kindness — he would not wish me to be happy so soon! Here she stopped for two or three minutes, earnestly looking upon him. Then resuming — My dearest cousin, said she, be comforted — what is dying but the common lot? The mortal frame may seem to labour — but that is all! — It is not so hard to die as I believed it to be. — The preparation is the difficulty — I bless God I have had time for that — the rest is worse to beholders than to me! I am all blessed hope — hope itself. She looked what she said, a sweet smile beaming over her countenance.

"After a short silence — Once more, my dear cousin, said she, but still in broken accents, commend me most dutifully to my father and mother. — There she stopped. And then proceeding — To my sister, to my brother, to my uncles — and tell them, I bless them with my parting breath — for all their goodness to me — even for their displeasure, I bless them — most happy has been to me my punishment here! Happy indeed! She was silent for a few moments, lifting up her eyes, and the hand her cousin held not between his. Then O death! said she, where is thy sting! (the words I remember to have heard in the burial-service read over my uncle and poor Belton). And after a pause — It is good for me that I was afflicted! Words of Scripture, I suppose. Then turning towards us, who were lost in speechless sorrow — O dear, dear gentlemen, said she, you know not what foretastes, — what assurances — and there she again stopped, and looked up as if in a thankful rapture, sweetly smiling.

"Then turning her head towards me—Do you, sir, tell your friend that I forgive him! And I pray to God to forgive him! Again pausing, and lifting up her eyes, as if praying that he would. Let him know how happily I die:—and that, such as my own, I wish to be his last hour. She was again silent a few moments: and then resuming—My sight fails me!—Your voices only—(for we both applauded her Christian, her divine frame, though in accents as broken as her own) and the voice of grief is alike in all. Is not this Mr. Morden's hand? pressing one of his with that he had just let go—Which is Mr. Belford's? holding out the other. I gave her mine. God Almighty bless you both, said she, and make you both—in your last hour—for you must come to this—happy as I am.

"She paused again, her breath growing shorter; and after a few minutes—And now, my dearest cousin, give me your hand—nearer—still nearer—drawing it towards her; and she pressed it with her dying lips—God protect you, dear, dear sir, and once more receive my best and most grateful thanks—and tell my dear Miss Howe, and vouchsafe to see and to tell my worthy Norton—she will be one day, I fear not, though now lowly in her fortunes, a saint in heaven—tell them both that I remember them with thankful blessings in my last moments! And pray God to give them happiness here for many, many years for the sake of their friends and lovers; and a heavenly crown hereafter; and such assurances of it, as I have, through the all-satisfying merits of our blessed Redeemer.

"Her sweet voice and broken periods methinks still fill my ears, and never will be out of my memory. And after a short silence, in a more broken and faint accent

—And you, Mr. Belford, pressing my hand, may God preserve you, and make you sensible of all your errors— you see, in me, how all ends — may you be — and down sank her head upon her pillow, she fainting away and drawing from us her hands. We thought she was then gone; and each gave way to a violent burst of grief. But soon showing signs of returning life, our attention was again engaged; and I besought her, when a little recovered, to complete in my favour her half-pronounced blessing. She waved her hand to us both, and bowed her head six times, as we have since recollected, as if distinguishing every person present, not forgetting the nurse and the maid-servant; the latter having approached the bed, weeping, as if crowding in for the divine lady's last blessing; and she spoke falteringly and inwardly — Bless — bless — bless you all —and—now—and now—(holding up her almost lifeless hands for the last time)—Come—O come—Blessed Lord Jesus! and with these words, the last but half-pronounced, expired:—such a smile, such a charming serenity overspreading her sweet face at the instant, as seemed to manifest her eternal happiness already begun. O Lovelace!—But I can write no more!"

The reader is of course free to form his own judgment upon this famous and often-praised scene. For my own part I am bound to confess that, while I realize its power and its pathos, I still feel that it lacks the crowning merit of simplicity. The art of it is too deliberate and too apparent. Belford is too obviously aware of the dramatic possibilities of the situation, and too evidently determined to get the maximum amount of effect out of it. To put the matter baldly, he writes it up. Moreover, he strikes a false note at the start: "As thou usedst to like my descriptions, I will give thee the woful scene that presented itself to me as I approached the bed." This at once suggests artifice. And though we must not indeed complain that poor Clarissa, like the reprobate Merry Monarch, "takes an unconscionable time in dying," we may still urge that, true to the business-like habits in which Richardson had manifestly trained her, and which she does not forget even at the end, she distributes her blessings and last wishes in far too methodical a fashion.

Regarded on the technical side, *Clarissa* is marred by one fundamental defect. The improbabilities of the plot are numerous and glaring. It has often been pointed out that even in the eighteenth century Lovelace could never have carried out his nefarious schemes unmolested. Law and justice were relatively weak at the time, it is true; but still they existed; and when Richardson requires us to believe that his drama of abduction could be successfully played in the hole-and-corner secrecy necessitated by his purposes, he makes greater demands upon us than, with all the willingness in the world, we are able to concede. That Lovelace, the clever and accomplished villain, should take all sorts of people, some of them obviously untrustworthy, into his confidence in respect to a crime which was then punishable by death, is also incredible. The consistency of Clarissa's character, moreover, is outraged for the sake of the action. Surely any one in her circumstances would have seized the first opportunity of throwing herself upon the protection of a magistrate. Such an opportunity presents itself when she makes her escape to Hampstead. But the intervention of a magistrate (say, Justice Fielding, as Scott suggests) would not only have ruined Lovelace' plot but would also have brought Richardson's story to a premature and unintended close. Hence the one thing that Clarissa ought to have done and would have done is precisely the one thing which she never dreams of doing.

In mere construction, therefore, *Clarissa*, though much more elaborate than *Pamela*, is almost as defective. In ethics, on the other hand, it is an immense advance upon that work. The theme is substantially the same; but here there is no question of virtue being "rewarded" in any worldly sense. The moral power of the narrative lies in its sympathetic delineation of piety, patience, courage, and resignation.

Clarissa, as Richardson himself said, is "a truly Christian heroine," who rises "superior to her trials." Noble she is throughout; but nowhere does she show her nobility to greater advantage than when she rejects her seducer's proposal that by the convention of marriage she shall connive with him in his sin. This is immeasurably better than Pamela and her coach-and-six.

The character of Clarissa is of course the central element in the novel, and if we cannot go the whole length with admirers who maintain that she is the most living woman in fiction, we may admit that she is perhaps the most carefully and the most elaborately drawn. Richardson has spared no pains in his determination to present her complete — an ideal of Christian womanhood; and the result of his efforts is a marvel of minute and delicate portraiture. Yet if the figure of Clarissa stands out supreme, more interest after all attaches to that of Lovelace. Evidently our author was concerned to make his Iago dramatically worthy of his Desdemona, and he accordingly treats him with the same laborious solicitude. Lovelace is well educated, accomplished, witty, attractive; he has the manners of a "fine gentleman," and a power of personal fascination which enables him to

carry everything before him. Nor is he altogether bad. He has his redeeming qualities—
among them, oddly enough (though why
Richardson should have insisted so much on
this point is a puzzle), a genuine respect for
religion! But he is a shameless and irredeem-
able profligate, and for the gratification of his
passions he is capable of acting with incredible
perfidy, brutality, and callousness. Considering the part he has to play in the plot, it
was necessary, Scott urges, that the character
of Lovelace should be highly colored. Highly
colored it certainly is. Lovelace is indeed a
"dazzling monster," not a man. He grips
our imagination, but we never quite believe
in him. He has all the qualities requisite for a
great dramatic triumph except the one mysterious but indispensable quality of life.
Richardson in fact attempted in Lovelace a
task beyond his powers. He had not the
knowledge of life necessary to make such a
study in supreme villainy human and convincing, nor had he the intense creative imagination which is often independent of direct
experience and a substitute for it. But the
effort was a great one, and if the result be only
a qualified success, it would be churlish to
withhold the admiration to which even such
qualified success is entitled. It must also be

remembered to Richardson's credit that if he failed to produce a human being he at any rate gave to the world a permanent type. Lovelace is still familiar as a tradition and a symbol to people who have never read a line of *Clarissa* and know nothing in detail about the arch-scoundrel whose name they freely use to "point a moral" or to "adorn a tale."[1]

Before leaving *Clarissa* I may just note that the history of its composition illustrates the profound seriousness with which his work was treated both by Richardson himself and by his friends. The world of his imagination was absolutely real to him; he lived with his characters; and he and his correspondents discussed their motives and actions as if they had been men and women whom they had met and known in the flesh. When the first four volumes of *Clarissa* appeared, the inner circle of the author's admirers was thrown into consternation by the report that the catastrophe was to be tragic. Upon this the little great man, who held the threads of the heroine's

[1] There has been some discussion as to the possible original or originals of Lovelace. Leigh Hunt suggested that Richardson might have caught "the tone" of his "manners and language" from Colley Cibber and the notorious profligate, the Duke of Wharton (one of the patrons of the evangelical poet of *Night Thoughts*) But the coarse, merry, loose-tongued old Cibber could hardly have been much help to him, and it is now known that his relations with Wharton were very slight. I incline to think with Johnson that Lovelace is in the main an "expansion" of the "gay Lothario" (whose name has also become proverbial) in Rowe's *Fair Penitent*.

destiny in his hands, was implored to set the
inevitable at naught, and in deference to the
readers' already overwrought feelings, to contrive a "happy ending." But Richardson was
obdurate. He would consent neither to com-
pensate Clarissa for her sufferings nor to "save
the soul" of her betrayer. In thus steeling
his heart against the solicitations of his would-
be advisers, he showed that he had the conscience of the true dramatic artist. He
admitted to Lady Bradshaigh that he was
himself "sensibly touched" by some of the
scenes he had evoked. But he could not
interfere with the logic of events. The fate
of his characters was of their own making, and
therefore lay beyond his control.

VII

Richardson's third and last novel, *The History of Sir Charles Grandison,* was published
in eight volumes, in 1754, as a pendant to
Clarissa. He had been blamed for making
Lovelace too fascinating. As an offset and
corrective he therefore undertook to depict
"the character and actions of a man of true
honour"—"a man of religion and virtue; of
liveliness of spirit; accomplished and agreeable;
happy in himself and a blessing to others."
Grandison is in fact the male counterpart of

Clarissa. He is the Christian hero as she is the Christian heroine; the ideal embodiment of all the masculine, as she had been of all the feminine, excellences.

In introducing his new work Richardson might have anticipated Canning's Needy Knife Grinder, and exclaimed—"Story? God bless you, I have none to tell, sir." *Sir Charles Grandison* has little plot and no dramatic interest. It is simply a patient, elaborate study of character. Sir Charles is placed in "a variety of trying scenes"; but these are avowedly arranged for the purpose of showing how "all his actions are regulated by one steady principle." The novel is indeed a demonstration rather than a story—a homily with illustrations. The incidents derive their value from the light which they throw upon the various aspects of the hero's personality, which is thus presented from many points of view to the end that it may serve as a type and an example.

As a result the purely didactic element is even more prominent here than it had been in *Pamela* and *Clarissa*. The narrative is choked by moral discussion and disquisition. Every event is made the subject of lengthy conversations and edifying commentary. The drama perpetually waits till the ethical thesis suggested has been developed to the full. This explains why a "venerable old lady" referred to by Scott, when she "became subject to drowsy fits," chose to have *Sir Charles Grandison* read to her in preference to any other work; "because," she used to say, "should I drop asleep in the course of the reading, I am sure when I awake I shall have lost none of the story, but shall find the party where I left them, conversing in the cedar-parlour."

The plot, such as it is, may be thus epitomized: Harriett Byron is an orphan who lives with her uncle, Mr. Selby. At the time the narrative opens she is "just turned of twenty, but looks not more than seventeen." Her beauty is remarkable—it is the beauty of expression as well as of feature; and equally remarkable are her intellectual gifts, the charm of her manner, and the sweetness of her disposition. Among her admirers—and, as may be inferred from the premises, she has many—is a certain Sir Hargrave Pollexfen, a "handsome and genteel" man of twenty-eight or thirty, with pale complexion and "bold" eyes (which some might call "goggling"), vain of his person and voluble in speech. He is the villain of the drama—a second edition of Lovelace, but in comparison a very poor and ineffective rascal. He has his designs

upon Harriett, and as Richardson is apparently
unable to think of anything else, he reproduces
once again the machinery of abduction which
he had already employed in his other two
novels. By dint of trickery, Pollexfen contrives to carry the young lady away, and then
he attempts to force her into a marriage with
him. But he is not so successful as his predecessors, Mr. B. and Lovelace; for Harriett
is rescued from his clutches by Sir Charles
Grandison, who appears in the nick of time,
and by his gallant and chivalrous conduct
makes a telling first entrance on the stage he
is henceforth to dominate. Sir Charles and
Harriett of course fall in love with each other.
But here a complication arises. Sir Charles is
already half-engaged to a noble Italian lady,
Clementina della Porretta, whom he has met
on his travels, and whom indeed he has promised to marry if difficulties about nationality
and religion can be overcome. For a time the
main interest of the story is provided by Sir
Charles' relations with these two beautiful
and charming women, and if his behavior as a
lover is open to criticism on the ground of his
want of ardor and his too marked impartiality,
he is, as will be anticipated, always punc-
tiliously correct. Poor Clementina goes mad,
but presently recovers, and comes to England

to avoid an unwelcome proposal of marriage in her own country. But in the meantime, after much dallying and suspense, and an endless amount of talk, Sir Charles' decision is made, and Harriett, who has been mainly responsible for the active love making, becomes Lady Grandison. Then the two rivals — the successful and the defeated — vie with one another (what about Richardson's boasted knowledge of the "female heart"?) in interchanges of courtesy and almost superfeminine generosity.

A number of minor incidents connected with the doings of subordinate characters are grouped about this central action, and help to swell the work without however adding appreciably to its interest. These may here be disregarded. The reader will conclude from the outline given that *Sir Charles Grandison* is desperately dull. It is. But as I have said, Richardson's aim was not to write an amusing novel but to produce a full-length portrait of the "perfect gentleman." How far then has he succeeded in this great design?

Well, he has painted for us in minutest detail an absolute incarnation of all the virtues, who ought, as one of his French critics has irreverently declared, to be both stuffed and canonized. Sir Charles is as much a "dazzling monster" as Lovelace; he is every bit as unreal; but Lovelace is at least interesting in his unreality, while Sir Charles — the pompous, self-conscious, ceremonious, sententious Sir Charles, who never once steps down from his moral stilts, or forgets for a moment how good a man he is, and who wants only a halo to become a (very Protestant) saint — is a prig and a bore. Moreover, even if we could ever persuade ourselves to believe in him, we could not accept him, as Richardson intended us to accept him, as a working model. He is too perfect. Richardson was himself obliged to recognize the force of this objection, and urged in reply, first, that his hero had, after all, his little redeeming defects — such as a tendency to passion and pride; and secondly, that even a perfect example may be "accommodated to particular imitation." But his protest is futile; Sir Charles remains a creature altogether too bright and good "for human nature's daily food." In fact, this "glory of his sex" is too far removed in both character and circumstances from the everyday plane of life to serve as a pattern for conduct. His creator endows him with transcendent qualities of person and heart. He presents him to us as Adonis and Solomon rolled into one. The Admirable Crichton pales in luster beside him.

He is so handsome that "were kings to be chosen for beauty and majesty"—instead of being selected for their intellectual and moral superiority, as we know to have been always the case—then "Sir Charles Grandison would have very few competitors." His goodness "absolutely dazzles" his admiring friends. In company he throws every one else in the shade by his powers of conversation. His fascination is such that it casts a spell upon everybody who comes in contact with him. He dresses in faultless taste and his manners are impeccable. Of his innumerable accomplishments it is enough to say that he speaks the languages, sings well in a "mellow manly voice," and is reckoned "one of the finest dancers in England." He has his passions under absolute control. His well-balanced nature lifts him above the reach of those temptations to which common mortality is subjected. His rank, his wealth, his power give him advantages which ordinary people like ourselves can never hope to enjoy. Such a man is one of the favored of the gods. The kind fairies have lavished all their choicest gifts upon him at his birth. The stars in their courses conspire in his behalf. He is too much of an exception to be taken as a rule. We may admire him at a distance; we may envy him (though

I do not think it in the least likely that we shall do one or the other); but to walk in his footsteps—that is out of the question.

Dismissing this adverse criticism, however, let me just touch upon one point of very great interest in this study of the "perfect gentleman." Dueling in Richardson's time was part of the recognized code of honor, and though Steele and Defoe had already attacked it, even so sturdy a moralist as Johnson found something to say in its defense. Now what should the "perfect gentleman" do in respect to this universal practice? The question was one which naturally came within the sphere of our author's didactic purpose, and he deserves high praise for the boldness with which he handled it. Sir Charles receives a challenge from Sir Hargrave Pollexfen, and to the amazement of Sir Hargrave and his friends he declines it; and this gives rise to an immense amount of discussion in which the whole matter is threshed out and the absurdity and wickedness of dueling are made abundantly clear. But here again it must be admitted that Sir Charles' circumstances are so exceptional that his solution of the problem in question can scarcely be said to apply to the case of the average man. He is able to act as he does without incurring the reproach of cowardice because, as Richardson was forced to admit, he has "both strength and skill to repel an affront" and at the same time to retain his "honour." He is, for example, an expert fencer, and his wonderful skill with the sword, as his engagement with the angry Mr. Fenwick shows, enables him easily to disarm his antagonist without inflicting any bodily injury. Intellectually, too, he is more than a match for his opponents. He beats them in argument from point to point. In a long interview on the subject which takes place between him and the Pollexfen party, one of these, a certain Mr. Bagenhall, who is a Roman Catholic, reminds him that the practice of dueling had been supported by some of the "famous casuists" of the church. Any other man than Sir Charles would have been silenced on this head by such an appeal to authority. But Sir Charles instantly rises to the occasion and shows that, Protestant though he is, he knows a great deal more about Roman Catholic opinion than Mr. Bagenhall himself.

"'Bannes and Cajetan, you mean. One a Spaniard, the other an Italian. But the highest authority of your church is full against them in this point. The Council of Trent treats the combatants who fall as self-murderers, and denies them Christian burial. It brands them, and all those who by their presence countenance and abet this shocking and unchristian practice with perpetual infamy, and condemns them to the loss of goods and estates. And furthermore, it deprives, *ipso jure*, all those sovereign princes who suffer such acts of violence to be perpetrated with impunity in the lands and cities which they hold of the church, of all the territories so held. I need not add to this that Louis XIV's edict against duelling was the greatest glory in his reign. And permit me to conclude with observing, that the base arts of poisoning by means of treacherous agents, and the cowardly practice of assassination by bravoes hired on purpose to wreak a private revenge so frequent in Italy, are natural *branches* of this old *Gothic tree*. And yet (as I have before hinted) the barbarous northern nations had pleas to make in behalf of duelling from *their* polity which we have not from *ours*, Christianity out of the question.'"

This of course settles the question so far as Mr. Bagenhall and Roman Catholic authority are concerned, and Sir Charles scores an easy victory. We, like his hearers, are much impressed by his erudition. But at the same time we remember that the ordinary English gentleman in a similar situation can hardly be expected to have the decrees of the Council of Trent and the edict of Louis XIV at his finger tips; and in this case the victory would inevitably go to Mr. Bagenhall by default.

But whatever we may think of Sir Charles Grandison to-day, he was in his own age taken very seriously as a practical study in moral perfection. This is amusingly shown by the two letters which Richardson appended "by desire" to the *Collection of Maxims* which he published in 1754. One of these was addressed "to a lady, who was solicitous for an additional volume . . . supposing" the *History* "ended abruptly, and expressing herself desirous to see Sir Charles in the parental character." This good woman, whose appetite for edification must have been insatiable, evidently regarded Richardson's novel as incomplete as a textbook of morality in one important respect. Her suggestion opened up possibilities which happily were never realized, for we might conceivably have had yet another continuation exhibiting Sir Charles as a grandfather. It was, however, reserved for Victor Hugo to write an *Art d'être grandpère*. The second letter was by way of answer to a friend "who had objected to Sir Charles Grandison's offer to allow his daughters by the Lady Clementina, had his marriage with her taken effect, to be educated Roman Catholics." The marriage, as we know did not "take effect," and it was surely scarcely worth while to make so much of a purely hypothetical case. But at this point Richardson was evidently regarded by zealous Protestants as having inculcated latitudinarian views.

VIII

I said at the outset of this essay that the modern reader recoils from Richardson's appalling prolixity, and I used the word prolixity advisedly. We often talk about the inordinate length of his novels. But I do not think, after all, that it is the mere length that we object to. There are plenty of long novels which we read with unflagging attention to the end and lay down at last with regret—*Don Quixote*, for example, *Monte Cristo*, *Pendennis*, *David Copperfield*. But in these the interest is kept alive by the variety and vivacity of the narrative and by what I may call the substantial quality of the materials which go to its composition. The enormous bulk of *Clarissa* and *Sir Charles Grandison*, on the other hand, is due to excessive elaboration—to the remorseless accumulation of details (often otiose), wearisome descriptions of unimportant things, endless repetitions, digressions, moralizings. These works are, therefore, swollen to their monstrous size not by the real mass of their matter but by the abuse of a particular method. The actual drama of *Clarissa* extends only from January 10 to December 8 —just eleven months; yet as we have seen, Richardson required seven volumes for its evolution.

222

Seven volumes for the affairs of less than a year!—this is writing history on a scale even more generous than that of Macaulay. One volume of the original eight-volume edition of *Sir Charles Grandison* is almost entirely occupied with getting Sir Charles and Harriett Byron married after all their difficulties have been surmounted; and the ordinary reader—the ordinary male reader, at any rate—can hardly be expected to share the enthusiasm of the two young ladies mentioned by Hazlitt, who copied out the whole description of Harriett's wedding clothes "for their own private gratification." Richardson is indeed as dilatory as life itself, and if we cannot quarrel with life because it is dull, we may justly quarrel with the art which reproduces too faithfully the dullness of life. "La nature," as D'Alembert admirably said, "est bonne à imiter, mais non pas jusqu'à l'ennui." And Richardson, if the truth must be told, is often *ennuyeux*. It is reported that one of his admirers solemnly informed him that with him prolixity had become a virtue. Yet it is a relief to know that even in his own day there were protests and complaints. "Such a multitude of reading," exclaimed a contemporary critic, "without coming at the story." And Johnson, with all his admiration for Richardson's art, was obliged to take stock of the same objection:

"Why, sir, if you were to read Richardson for the story, your impatience would be so fretted that you would hang yourself. You must read him for the sentiment, and consider the story only as giving rise to the sentiment."[1]

It must, however, be remembered that Richardson had the qualities of his defects, and that the special power which we are compelled to recognize in him was bound up with the prolixity which we deplore. His immense structures are built up with inexhaustible patience out of innumerable small and often trivial things. He proceeds by the rule of line upon line, and it is certain that he could have achieved his effects in no other way. His art is the art of the infinitely little. It is also, if the paradox may be allowed, the art of entire artlessness. He will not admit the difference between the essential and the non-essential. A character (like Mr. Singleton in *Sir Charles Grandison*) may appear for a moment only on the scene and then drop out of sight; but he is described as minutely as if he were destined to play an important part

[1] Here and there, however, a modern reader may be found whose impatience is not fretted by Richardson's longwindedness, but who, on the contrary, seems to enjoy it. "I like those great *still* books," Tennyson used to say, with regard to *Clarissa;* and again—"I wish there were a great novel in hundreds of volumes that I might go on and on."—(*Memoir,* II, 172).

in the story. Matters which have nothing
whatever to do with the real business in hand
are dwelt upon at length. Every conversation
has to be reported with literal accuracy.
Richardson's novels are utterly formless.
They sprawl out in every direction; the life
history of every person introduced is given
from the cradle; as in the old romances, which
he sought to displace, but from which he took
over much more than he realized, we continually get lost in labyrinths of episodes which
have little or no connection with the central
theme. We often grow weary of all this much
ado about nothing. Yet the fact remains
that by this diffuseness and by this very
disregard of all the canons of art, Richardson
does succeed in producing a curious illusion of
actual life. "There is," as Hazlitt put it with
his customary felicity, "an artificial reality
about his works which is nowhere else to be
met with." And this is the more remarkable
because of the absurdity of his plots, of which
I have already spoken, and the implausibility
of his method—the method of conducting his
story entirely by means of letters which pass
among its characters.

This "epistolary" method was at first, as
we have learned, a matter of accident only.
Richardson adopted it in *Pamela* simply

because *Pamela* was an offshoot from a Complete Letter Writer. But he continued to employ it in his later novels in part because of his own personal fondness for letter writing, and in part from artistic considerations.

These considerations are set forth in the preface to *Clarissa:*

"Much more lively and affecting must be the style of those who write in the height of the present distress, the mind tortured by the pangs of uncertainty, the events then hidden in the womb of time, than the dry narrative unanimated style of a person relating difficulties and dangers surmounted, the relater perfectly at ease; and if himself unmoved by his own story, then not likely greatly to affect the reader."

This is not well put, but the point of it is clear. Richardson claims for the novel-in-letters this advantage over the novel in either the ordinary third-personal or the autobiographical form, that it enables the persons of the drama themselves to relate its events, and to give expression to the feelings evoked by such events, at the time of their occurrence. Much might be said in reply to his argument; but we may still acknowledge a certain amount of theoretical justification for his claim. By the use of the epistolary method the novelist keeps us in intimate touch with his characters. We see everything from their different points of view. The incidents are detailed again and again, with comments and comments upon these comments, by those who take part or are directly interested in them; and if meanwhile the story stagnates, the motive-forces behind the story are fully revealed. It is indeed from the psychological side—the side with which Richardson was chiefly concerned—that the value of his method is most apparent.

At the same time its drawbacks are very obvious. An interchange of letters provides at best a cumbrous machinery for action. The interest of the story as story is too much scattered. That wholeness of view which naturally results from the ordinary methods of narration is under the conditions imposed by the epistolary form obtainable only by repetitions which become tiresome. Even on the psychological side such conditions operate as hindrances and limitations: as the author does not himself appear in person, he can never supplement the revelation of character given by the persons themselves or by those about them by analysis and commentary of his own. He thus creates for himself gratuitously the difficulties which are inherent in the drama but are really foreign to the looser art of the novel. But worst of all is the extreme artificiality of the device. It is impossible for us to accept all this everlasting letter writing. The letters have to be written because the story has to be carried on, and they are therefore written in season and out of season. For the same reason they are filled with lengthy descriptions of places and people, minute reports of incidents, verbatim records of conversations, and all sorts of other matters which would enter into an ordinary narrative as of course, but which no one would dream of putting into his correspondence. Richardson's characters, small and great, cultured and uncultured, his Pamela no less than his Clarissa, his Lovelace no less than his Grandison, whatever their stations, their business, their temperaments, have one and all the author's own mania for letter writing; one and all, too, they have his own fatal facility with the pen; one and all, be their circumstances ever so pressing, they have likewise unlimited leisure. They write at all times, even the most unlikely; in moments of crisis, when their fate literally hangs in the balance, they still have strength of mind and self-possession enough to write; watched, interrupted, harassed, interfered with, true to the main purpose of their existence, they yet contrive to write. Moreover, they keep copies and make minutes of their letters; they draw up documents which are submitted now to this person now to that for criticism and approval; shorthand writers are even concealed in closets to take full notes of conversations which, afterwards duly transcribed, are sent about under "covering" epistles and made the text of further correspondence. Richardson's world, in fact, as some one has said, resembles nothing so much as a large, well-ordered office, where everything is arranged, analyzed, docketed, filed away for future reference. As Hazlitt put it, "If the business of life consisted in letter writing, and was carried on by the post (like a Spanish game of chess) human nature would be what Richardson represents it." Richardson himself on one occasion sought to explain Pamela's itch for scribbling. He had much better have left the matter alone. He only drew attention to the absurdity by trying to excuse it.

Nor is the bulk of his letters less amazing than their number and frequency. On this point Sir Leslie Stephen once made an interesting calculation. He found that on March 22 Harriett Byron produced a letter of fourteen pages of print and two others of six and twelve pages respectively. These she followed up the next day with two more of eighteen and ten pages. On the 24th she wrote still two more, aggregating thirty pages; at the end of one of which she remarks that she is forced to lay down the pen, which however she takes up again to add six further pages by way of postscript. In three days, therefore, this industrious and facile lady, who meanwhile is of course occupied with the things about which she writes, turns out ninety-six pages of print—ninety-six pages!—a feat of which Scott himself need not have been ashamed. Macaulay estimated that the entire interest of her small fortune must have been consumed in the postage on these incessant and voluminous epistles.

I have often discussed this matter with warm admirers of our novelist and their contention is, that while it may be easy in this way to exhibit the radical falseness of his method, we are not really conscious of it while we are under the spell of one of his books. Are we not? On such a point I suppose the final appeal must be to personal experience, and for my part I must frankly confess that I am very conscious of it indeed. The fact that, as I am perfectly well aware, no human being could or would ever write such letters as Richardson requires us to accept as authentic, continually interferes with my interest in the alleged writers themselves. There is something factitious about it all from a sense of which I cannot escape.

IX

In the foregoing pages frequent reference has been made to Richardson's didacticism. The subject is, however, so important for a proper understanding of the man and his work that I must return to it for a moment here.

That he regarded himself primarily as a moralist is sufficiently clear from the whole tenor of his writings. But lest his readers might still be in some doubt as to his aims, he more than once defined his position with an emphasis which made misapprehension impossible. He wished, he declared, to have his books classed, not with ordinary fiction, but with Taylor's *Holy Living, The Practice of Piety,* and other treatises of the like character. "They appear," he explained, adopting the tone of apology, "in the humble guise of a novel only by way of accommodation to the manners and tastes of an age overwhelmed with luxury and abandoned to sound and senselessness." And again, with reference to *Sir Charles Grandison:* "From what has been premised, it may be supposed that the present collection is not published ultimately, nor even principally, any more than the other two, for the sake of entertainment only. A much nobler end is in view." He wrote

231

throughout, then, in the hope that "truth embodied in a tale" might "enter in at lowly doors." His paramount object was edification, and that object was never for a moment allowed to drop out of sight. The story itself is but the gilding of the pill.

It is possible of course for a writer of fiction to be didactic without actually mounting the pulpit and turning his work into a sermon. The artist who is really an artist will indeed be careful to avoid the professional pose; he will be satisfied in the main with the indirect inculcation of the ideas he wishes to convey and will use the direct method with caution and only occasionally. But Richardson knew nothing of this kind of reticence. He never leaves his moral to take care of itself. He thrusts it perpetually to the front. In his anxiety lest it should be missed, he underscores it heavily and loads it with emphasis. Every incident is made the text for a homily and every movement of the plot furnishes subject matter for commentary, warning, advice. Hence the everlasting intrusion of ethical discussion upon the narrative; hence the direct exhortation; hence the many, many pages of commonplace reflection and moralizings which, however well-meant, often degenerate into downright twaddle. The modern novel reader can hardly be blamed if he takes Richardson at his word and does class his writings with *Holy Living* and *The Practice of Piety*—with results which need scarcely be specified.

If further proof be required of our author's constant preoccupation with his didactic aims it will be found in his supplementary volume to which I have already referred, though as a matter of convenience I then cited it under an abbreviated name. Its full title, which must now be given, runs: *A Collection of the Moral and Instructive Sentiments, Maxims, Cautions, and Reflections, contained in the Histories of Pamela, Clarissa, and Sir Charles Grandison, digested under their Proper Heads.* Richardson's object in preparing this compendium was, so to speak, to reduce the scattered teachings of the said "Histories" into a regular manual of conduct. The matter is therefore systematically arranged; cases in point are given from the novels to enforce the rules laid down; and for the reader's further assistance, a very full index is provided. Thus, *s.v. Fortitude*, the following highly original precept is offered: "It becomes a good person in distress to make a virtue of necessity, and to try to bring real good out of seeming evil." Then comes the "case" in support: "See Pamela's example in deep calamity for the illustration of this doctrine." Richardson, it is evident, must have been tremendously impressed by the ethical value of his work to make it in this way the basis of a practical handbook of morality. His *Collection* is doubtless very instructive. Unfortunately, it labors under the disadvantage of being a trifle ridiculous.

But what of the character of his moral teaching? In answering this question we need not now go beyond generalities, and it will therefore be enough to say that it is marked by much the same qualities and limitations as we have already noted in dealing with the moral teaching of Lillo. Like Lillo, Richardson represents the rising power of the middle classes in literature. Like Lillo, he voices the protest of the middle classes against the lingering traditions of aristocratic corruption. At a time when, despite the excellent work which had been done shortly before by Defoe, Addison, and Steele, it was still "good form" to be a rake, to treat women as playthings, and to scoff openly at decency and the marriage vow,[1] he made it his chief concern to exhibit the evils of profligacy and the sanctity of the

1 We learn on the authority of *The Connoisseur* that in 1755 "the kept mistress" was still "a constant part of the retinue of the fine gentleman" and was "indeed as indispensable a part of his equipage as a French *valet-de-chambre* or a four-wheeled post-chaise."

domestic virtues; and if there is something oppressive and unwholesome—something too much suggestive of a hothouse—about the atmosphere of his books—if in *Pamela* in particular his moral is developed in a way which seems to us both crude and offensive, we must remember that in his case, as in the parallel case of Lillo, his work can be properly appreciated only when it is put back into the setting of his age. All the ideals and sentiments surviving in the degenerate chivalry of the upper classes—as, for example, in their extravagant gallantry and their so-called code of honor—are repudiated by Richardson root and branch. His criticism of life is dictated by sound good sense no less than by genuine piety. His morality rests upon the firm basis of religion, but it is at the same time a morality of the counting-house—sober, practical, utilitarian.

It is from this point of view that we can best understand the fundamentally democratic character of his novels. On this matter, it is true, an erroneous opinion may easily be formed. We have seen that Richardson shared the ordinary eighteenth-century tradesman's feelings of respect for the aristocracy, and that these feelings to some extent color his work. This fact may itself mislead us. It is also noteworthy that though he began in the most radical way by making a mere lady's maid the heroine of a novel, he never repeated this daring experiment. On the contrary, he showed a tendency to rise in the social scale; his Clarissa being a young lady of "good" though not noble family, and his Sir Charles Grandison, a man of position as well as fortune. Yet directly and indirectly the tendency of his teaching was democratic because his spirit to the last was the spirit of the middle classes, and because throughout he made the individual character supreme and treated rank and all its attendant advantages as secondary and adventitious. The iron barrier which social convention had set up between Pamela and her master is at length broken down by Pamela's virtue. Lovelace's birth and breeding, his wealth and accomplishments, serve only to make his vices the more conspicuous and the more appalling. The real greatness of Sir Charles inheres in the fact, not that he is *Sir* Charles, but that he is what any one, high or low, rich or poor, may be if he likes — a "man of true honor," in whom character gives dignity to position, not position to character. Here and there, too, Richardson strikes the distinctively democratic note. When, for instance, Pamela hears that her master may be made a peer, her reply is that it would be better if he were made a virtuous man.

X

For reasons which our little study will have made apparent, the enjoyment of Richardson is now almost a lost taste. His plots are so clumsy, his machinery is so absurd, his method is so tiresome, his moralizings are so obtrusive, his diffusiveness is so terrible, that it is extremely difficult for us to-day to do justice to his real powers. It is well, therefore, that we should remind ourselves in closing that, whatever our own private judgment may be, his historical importance is very great. He opened an entirely new chapter in the annals of our prose fiction, and partly by what he himself accomplished and partly by the inspiration which he gave to others, he laid the foundations of our modern novel. His enormous vogue on the continent of Europe, moreover, entitles him to be regarded as one of the most influential English writers of the eighteenth century. *Pamela* and *Clarissa* made the tour of Europe, and *Clarissa* in particular was one of the works which carried the newly awakened spirit of the English middle classes far and wide through many lands. In France, Diderot went into raptures over it and placed its author beside Moses, Homer, Sophocles, and Euripides, while Rousseau pronounced it the finest novel in the world and fashioned his own *Julie* upon it. In Germany, it powerfully affected Lessing, Goethe, and a host of minor writers, for whom Richardson was, in Gellert's phrase, "the magician," and it became a potent force in early German romanticism. A Dutch minister declared that parts of it, if found in the Bible, would be quoted as proofs of divine inspiration. Even Russia felt the subtle spell of Salisbury Court and Fulham. Karamsin proclaimed Richardson as "the most artistic painter of man's moral nature" the world had ever seen, and took *Pamela* as the model of his own once-famous *Poor Louisa*.

This is a wonderful record. You and I may yawn over the little printer's countless pages. But we must not forget that our forefathers wept over them. We may even let the dust gather on his books. But those same books were once intensely alive. Tastes change, and the glamour of Richardson is now a thing of the past. To revive it is impossible. But his place in literature is secure.